The Scarecrow Author Bibliographies

NORMAN MAILER:

A Comprehensive Bibliography

compiled by
LAURA ADAMS

with an introduction by
ROBERT F. LUCID

The Scarecrow Author Bibliographies, No. 20

THE SCARECROW PRESS, INC.
Metuchen, N. J.   1974

Library of Congress Cataloging in Publication Data

Adams, Laura.
   Norman Mailer: a comprehensive bibliography.

   (The Scarecrow author bibliographies, no. 20)
   1. Mailer, Norman--Bibliography.
Z8543.65.A3   016.813'5'4   74-17163
ISBN 0-8108-0771-8

For all of us who needed this book

TABLE OF CONTENTS

PREFACE

by Laura Adams

Not until the compilation of this bibliography was nearly completed did I realize how extensive it would be. When I began research on Mailer for my dissertation in 1970 it was clear that few had written seriously or extensively of his work. Reviews and biographical pieces made up--and still do--the bulk of secondary sources. Since that time, however, the scholarship industry has geared up and launched into full Mailer production. More than thirty dissertations dealing in whole or in part with his work now exist, as well as a growing number of books where none existed before 1969, and scholarly articles.

The tide of critical attention began to turn in 1968 with the publication of The Armies of the Night, reaching its crest in 1969 when Armies was awarded both the National Book Award and the Pulitzer Prize. In short, Mailer became respectable. If scholars are still slow to accept the Mailer personality, the Mailer canon is now, after more than a quarter-century and not a little ironically, solidly establishment. And so the time is ripe for this reference work.

The present volume is reasonably complete through 1973 (with some entries for 1974 as well) with certain exceptions. Mailer's works published abroad are not included, nor was criticism not in English exhaustively accumulated, although enough is present to indicate the interest the Japanese, Italians, and English take in Mailer. The list of anthologies reprinting

Mailer originals remains incomplete since the necessary information was not available from Mailer's publishers (with the exceptions of Little, Brown and the New American Library, to which I am grateful) or his literary agent because of the enormity of work involved in digging it up. Originally, too, I had intended to include a list of Mailer's television appearances, mainly on the talk show circuit, but unfortunately no records of these appearances exist, other than a large bowl of undated excerpts in Mailer's Brooklyn Heights residence. Finally, I included some partial secondary source citations on the reasoning that part of an omission is preferable to a complete one.

By way of restitution for whatever omissions and errors the reader may discover, I have included a list of Mailer's unpublished manuscripts whose existence was virtually unknown until now. Most are short stories written during the early 1940's, during Mailer's Harvard and Army days, along with the two novels, No Percentage and A Transit to Narcissus. Other major finds include the original (Rinehart) version of The Deer Park in cut galleys (which Carol Holmes has used to prepare a variorum edition of the novel) and two movie treatments on which Mailer collaborated during a short stay in Hollywood. All of these materials are located in Mailer's vault in Manhattan, thanks largely to the efforts of Robert F. Lucid, whose introduction, narrating the way in which the papers came to be collected, follows.

Although I have listed only those unpublished works which are finished in some sense and therefore theoretically publishable, the vault contains boxes upon boxes, quite literally, of manuscripts genetic of published works, research materials for books such as Of a Fire on the Moon, memorabilia, clippings, and odd scraps of paper calculated to produce nightmares in bibliographers. Mailer is given to notetaking in mini-spirals and to jotting down thoughts or poems on the backs of bills and laundry receipts. Given these circumstances and the fact that the vault is neither air conditioned, dust-free nor adequately lit, I chose the simplest alternative. A full inventory of Mailer's papers must await a hardier scholar.

No one prepares a comprehensive bibliography without relying on the spadework of others. I wish to acknowledge all those whose bibliographies have supplied items for this one, including Donald Kaufmann, one of the first Mailer scholars, Douglas Shepard, B. A. Sokoloff, Mike Lennon, and especially Robert F. Lucid, whose checklist of primary sources was invaluable.

To the Liberal Arts Research Committee of Wright State University, who financed my adventures in Mailer's vault, and to Norman Mailer and Bob Lucid who made it possible, I owe thanks. And again to Bob Lucid I am most grateful for his splendid introduction to this volume and for his many other generosities.

To all who use this book, may your studies flourish.

Wright State University
January, 1974

INTRODUCTION

by Robert F. Lucid

Perhaps it is not too risky to assume that any-
one who is looking at this book is well beyond the
stage of requiring an introduction either to Norman
Mailer in particular or to the virtues of itemized bibliography in general. My purpose here is to give the
reader some idea of the present state of the Mailer
papers, and the easiest, if not necessarily the best
way to do this, is to recount in somewhat autobio-
graphical fashion how the papers came to be assembled.

In the Spring of 1958 Mailer came to the University of Chicago for a brief stint as a visiting writer,
and I, in my first year of teaching, helped play host
to him there. For a week or so I tried to keep pace
with him as he pursued his many interests, and we
became friends. The subject of literary papers did not
come up at that time, nor did we discuss it in the few
social letters we exchanged over the next year. In
1959, about the time I left Chicago to go teach at
Wesleyan, Advertisements for Myself came out, and
in letters about the book we said that since I was now
in the East we ought to be getting together.

Some difficult years followed, but he sometimes
came to Wesleyan to give talks (one was right after
the death of JFK, and during the whole visit it was as
if everyone had been given huge injections of novocaine)
and we kept in touch. After I switched universities
and came to work at Penn, however, I saw more of
Mailer. I was travelling a lot on a moonlighting job

and, by 1965 or so, had developed a habit of visiting Mailer's various residences. He has an excellent brown-stone apartment building in Brooklyn and his parents live in Brooklyn too; at various times he rented various houses in Provincetown as well as else-where in New England, and of course the man is a famously hospitable host. I would vacation with my wife and son or stop over on business trips or just show up. As friends we took an interest in each other's families and finances and work problems, and I used to spend a fair amount of time poking through his large and scattered library. At first it was just browsing, but after a time it became a matter of fol-lowing his reading, going over with some care books which he had read and annotated, and sometimes talk-ing with him about this.

But the point is that in addition to books I regu-larly came upon randomly shelved letters, notebooks, drafts of manuscripts, finished manuscripts, and cor-rected and uncorrected proof sheets. For someone who was supposed to have been trained in scholarship I was remarkably slow in realizing that I had a quite real responsibility to see to it that this material wasn't lost, as it was certainly in danger of being. Finally, though, I came to see how it was. Every available spare storage inch in the comfortable but small apartment occupied by Mailer's parents was al-ready crammed with parcels wrapped in brown paper. In these, going all the way back to his childhood, were files and letters and essays, schoolwork and juvenilia, and there were huge scrapbooks documenting the first days of big success lovingly put together by his par-ents. But the apartment was just too small to hold all that there was, and the rest was scattered all over (except for the final manuscript of The Naked and the Dead, which the Yale University library had asked for early and which the flattered young author, of course, had handed right over).

In a tiny office on the third floor of the Brook-lyn apartment building Mailer's secretary worked under the looming shadows of great filing cabinets, all of them bulging with correspondence, business papers, and notebooks containing outlines, ideas, sketches, phone numbers, everything. Stuffed in among these would be more manuscripts, mostly but by no means always already published, and also there were basements and attics and garages, all with important material tossed into them. It seemed obvious that a good way to pass spare vacation and visiting time would be to work through all this and get it into one safe place.

Two years later the job was, at least after a fashion, completed. I would work with a kind of sporadic steadiness, finally shuttling with some regularity between Philadelphia and New York whether Mailer was at home or not (The American Philosophical Society took an interest in the project and offered a small grant for transportation and minor expenses). In summer I would return from Provincetown with extra papers in among the suitcases, and the heavier things I would ship to Brooklyn. There, in separate cardboard boxes which were each about the size of a double apple box, were assembled the working papers --from first drafts and notes through corrected and final page proofs--of each of Mailer's published volumes. Other boxes contained manuscripts and working papers for uncollected and unpublished things. There were boxes of periodicals containing Mailer pieces, boxes filled with secondary material, letter files, business files, journals and other private papers. Cassette tapes (which for the most part have yet to be transcribed) were recorded to itemize the things in each box. Many boxes have been added since, but after the first two years there were thirty-six of those big containers, all full, extending in time up through a collection of materials concerning Of a Fire on the Moon.

A fireproof storage vault slotted onto the bed of a warehouse truck was summoned out to Brooklyn, and one long afternoon two truckers and I, supervised by Mailer's mother, loaded the truck, made up a map of what was arranged inside, and sent the vehicle off. It was driven back downtown, the vault was unslotted

xiii

and hoisted into its place on an aisle in a big storage building, and I go down there periodically and put in the new material which, of course, keeps coming.

A bibliography reader could see, as perhaps a general reader could not, how much fun it was. The quickest pleasure was in the chase, finding the plaster-buried, mouse-nibbled manuscript of The Deer Park in a basement tool bench drawer in Brooklyn, or discovering and identifying and then spending long nights reading through the unpublished work listed here in the bibliography. Once I found an uncashed check for several hundred dollars, the payment for an old Book Week article. Court transcripts of the trials of Lenny Bruce would brush elbows with materials Mailer had written in support of the 1948 Henry Wallace presidential campaign, and there was a complete file of those extraordinary early Village Voice columns. A beautiful woman (picture enclosed) had submitted an invitation in the form of a Christmas card, and this emerged like a kind of pop-out mobile from among the leaves of a somber essay on the policy of Western defense. It was a pleasure.

Itemizing the individual details onto cassettes was the hard work, of course, and often wasn't a pleasure at all, but it was great when something totally unsuspected would emerge. By reading with care for the tape I broke the code of Mailer's acrostic poem "The Drunk's Bebop and Chowder," and in the grind of detailing the Esquire file I found a wonderful collection of letters to the editor. One fine thing came from examining pages from an unpublished essay Mailer had begun after he and his wife, Beverly Bentley, had driven out to Las Vegas to cover the second Patterson-Liston fight. The essay describes a long drive, a stopover with an old Army friend who was a doctor, and describes further the observing of an autopsy on the body of a man who had had cancer but who went out fast from a burst appendix. The typescript is reworked in Mailer's hand, changing the "we" who took the trip to "I"; changing it, that is, to an experience undergone by Steve Rojack, the hero of An American

Dream. The epilogue in the novel as finally published was in fact the beginning of the novel as composed, and this was discovered only when the manuscript pages were being described onto the cassette. Itemizing the vast working drafts of An American Dream, on the other hand, was a nightmare. None of the hundreds of pages of typescript is paginated, the pages are mixed together at random, and I never did get them separated out correctly.

The comforts and discomforts of compilation aside, of course, the significant thing is that the archive exists. Some scholars have used it already: Carol Holmes has been working on a variorum edition of The Deer Park which ought to be completed soon, and of course Laura Adams came in to itemize the unpublished manuscripts. The thousands of letters, though, and the journals and other private papers make the collection sufficiently confidential so that its real use will be as a center for future rather than present scholarly activity. Still, readers of a bibliography as detailed and ambitious as this one are sure to be pleased at the knowledge that the great majority of the Mailer papers have been and are being preserved.

University of Pennsylvania
January, 1974

CHRONOLOGY

1923   Born January 31 at Long Branch, New Jersey
          to Isaac Barnett ("Barney") Mailer and
          Fanny Schneider Mailer.

1939   Graduates from Boys' High School, Brooklyn,
          New York.
          Enters Harvard University.

1941   Wins Story magazine's annual contest with "The
          Greatest Thing in the World."

1943   Graduates from Harvard with B. S. with honors
          in aeronautical engineering.

1944   Marries Beatrice Silverman.
          Inducted into U. S. Army.

1946   Discharged from Army after serving with 112th
          Cavalry in Leyte, Luzon, and Japan.

1947   Studies at the Sorbonne on G. I. bill.

1948   The Naked and the Dead published.
          Campaigns for Henry Wallace and Progressive
          Party.

1949   Tries scriptwriting in Hollywood.
          First child, Susan, born.

1951   Barbary Shore published.

1952   Divorced from Beatrice Silverman.

1954   Marries Adele Morales.

1955   The Deer Park published.

1957   Second child, Danielle, born.
        The White Negro published.

1959   Advertisements for Myself published.
        Third child, Elizabeth Anne, born.

1960   Announces intention of running for Mayor of
            New York.
        Stabs wife.

1962   Deaths for the Ladies and other disasters pub-
            lished.
        Divorced from Adele Morales.
        Marries Lady Jean Campbell.
        Fourth child, Kate, born.
        Begins monthly column, "The Big Bite," for
            Esquire.

1963   The Presidential Papers published.
        Divorced from Lady Jean Campbell.
        Marries Beverly Bentley.

1964   An American Dream appears in Esquire, Janu-
            ary-August.
        Fifth child, Michael Burks, born.

1965   An American Dream published.
        Addresses Modern Language Association.

1966   Cannibals and Christians published.
        Sixth child, Stephen McLeod, born.

1967   The Deer Park produced off Broadway.
        The Deer Park: A Play published.
        Wild 90 (film) premieres.
        The Bullfight published.
        The Short Fiction of Norman Mailer published.
        Why Are We in Vietnam? published.
        Elected to the National Institute of Arts and
            Letters

Participates in the march on the Pentagon.

1968   Beyond the Law (film) premieres.
        The Idol and the Octopus published.
        The Armies of the Night published.
        Covers political conventions.
        Miami and the Siege of Chicago published.
        Maidstone filmed.

1969   Runs for Democratic nomination for Mayor of
            New York.
        Wins Pulitzer Prize and National Book Award
            for The Armies of the Night.
        Covers first manned moonshot.
        Receives honorary Doctor of Letters degree from
            Rutgers University.

1970   Of a Fire on the Moon published.
        Maidstone premieres.

1971   The Prisoner of Sex published.
        "King of the Hill" published.
        Maidstone: A Mystery published.
        Seventh child, Maggie Alexandra, born to
            Carol Stevens.

1972   Existential Errands published.
        Covers political conventions.
        St. George and the Godfather published.
        Isaac B. Mailer dies.

1973   Holds fiftieth birthday party.
        Introduces Fifth Estate concept.
        Marilyn published.
        Receives Macdowell Colony award.

1974   The Faith of Graffiti published.
        Works on new novel.

I. PRIMARY SOURCES

A. BOOKS

(Note: The publisher(s) of current paperback
reprints are given in brackets.)

The Naked and the Dead. New York: Rinehart, 1948
[Signet, Rinehart]. Novel.

Barbary Shore. New York: Rinehart, 1951 [Signet].
Novel.

The Deer Park. New York: G. P. Putnam's, 1955
[Berkeley]. Novel.

The White Negro: Superficial Reflections on the Hipster. San Francisco: City Lights, 1957 [paper-
back only]. Essay. Reprinted from Dissent
(Summer, 1957), 276-293 and in Advertisements
for Myself.

Advertisements for Myself. New York: G. P. Putnam's, 1959 [Berkeley]. Miscellany.

Deaths for the Ladies and other disasters. New York:
G. P. Putnam's, 1962 [Grove Press, Signet].
Poems. Preface reprinted in Existential Errands.

The Presidential Papers. New York: G. P. Putnam's,
1963 [Berkeley]. Miscellany.

An American Dream. New York: Dial, 1965 [Dell].
Novel.

1

Cannibals and Christians. New York: Dial, 1966
    [Delta, Dell]. Miscellany.

The Bullfight: A Photographic Narrative with Text by
    Norman Mailer. New York: C.B.S. Legacy
    Books, Macmillan, 1967. Essay, photographs,
    and recording.

The Deer Park: A Play. New York: Dial, 1967.
    Play, with introduction reprinted in Existential
    Errands.

The Short Fiction of Norman Mailer. New York:
    Dell, 1967 [paperback only]. Previously published
    fiction with preface that is reprinted in Existential
    Errands.

Why Are We in Vietnam? New York: G. P. Putnam's,
    1967 [Berkeley]. Novel.

The Idol and the Octopus: Political Writings by Nor-
    man Mailer on the Kennedy and Johnson Admin-
    istrations. New York: Dell, 1968 [paperback
    only]. Essays with new introduction that is re-
    printed in Existential Errands.

The Armies of the Night: The Novel as History/
    History as a Novel. New York: New American
    Library, 1968 [Signet]. On 1967 march on the
    Pentagon.

Miami and the Siege of Chicago. New York: New
    American Library, 1968 [Signet]. On 1968 politi-
    cal conventions.

Of a Fire on the Moon. Boston: Little, Brown, 1970
    [Signet]. On 1969 manned moonflight.

"King of the Hill." New York: Signet, 1971 [paper-
    back only]. Reprinted from "Ego," Life, March
    19, 1971, pp. 18f, 19, 22-30, 32, 36, and in
    Existential Errands. Essay on Muhammed Ali.

Maidstone: A Mystery. New York: Signet, 1971
    [paperback only]. Essay on, text of and stills
    from Maidstone film.

The Prisoner of Sex. Boston: Little, Brown, 1971
    [Signet]. Essay.

Existential Errands. Boston: Little, Brown, 1972
    [Signet]. Miscellany.

St. George and the Godfather. New York: New
    American Library, 1972 [paperback only]. On
    1972 political conventions.

Marilyn: A Novel Biography. New York: Grosset
    and Dunlap, 1973. Novel biography with photo-
    graphs.

The Faith of Graffiti. New York: Praeger, 1974.
    Essay to accompany photographs.

B. PERIODICAL PIECES AND PREFACES

Note: Reprintings will be indicated by these abbreviations of the works in which they appear:

AM: Advertisements for Myself

PP: The Presidential Papers

DL: Deaths for the Ladies and other disasters

CC: Cannibals and Christians

SF: The Short Fiction of Norman Mailer

IO: The Idol and the Octopus

EE: Existential Errands

RM: Running Against the Machine, ed. Peter Manso.

1938 "Model Airplanes." Physical Scientist [Boys' High School, Brooklyn], December, 1938, unpaginated.

1941 "The Greatest Thing in the World." Harvard Advocate, April, 1941, pp. 3-6, 24-28. Story. Reprinted in Story, November-December, 1941, pp. 17-26 and in AM and SF.

1942 "Right Shoe on Left Foot." Harvard Advocate, May, 1942, pp. 12-18, 30-33. Story.

"Maybe Next Year." Harvard Advocate, May, 1942, pp. 25-27. Story. Reprinted in AM and SF.

4

1944   "A Calculus at Heaven."   Cross Section: A Collection of American Writing, ed. Edwin Sea-
ver.   New York: McClellan, 1944, pp. 60-81.
Novella.   Reprinted in AM and SF.   [Original
working title, "The Foundation."]

1948   "Do Professors Have Rights?"   New York Post,
October 8, 1948, pp. 5, 34.   Article.

1951   "The Defense of the Compass."   The Western
Defenses, ed. Sir John George Smyth.   London: Allan Wingate, 1951.   Essay.

1952   "Our Country and Our Culture," in "America and
the Intellectuals."   Partisan Review (Summer,
1952), 298-301.   Symposium contribution.
Reprinted in AM.

"The Paper House."   New World Writing II.
New York: New American Library, 1952,
pp. 58-59.   Story.   Reprinted in AM and SF.

"The Dead Gook."   Discovery #1, ed. John W.
Aldridge and Vance Bourjaily.   New York:
Pocket Books, 1952, pp. 56-76.   Story.
Reprinted in AM and SF.

1953   "The Notebook."   Cornhill, 1953, pp. 166, 481-
84.   Story.   Reprinted in The Berkeley Book
of Modern Writing No. III, ed. William
Phillips and Philip Rahv.   New York:
Berkeley, 1956, pp. 106-09; and in The
Literary Guide and Rationalist Review [Lon-
don], January, 1954, pp. 13-14 and in AM
and SF.

1953   "The Language of Men."   Esquire, April, 1953,
pp. 61, 115-17.   Story.   Reprinted in AM
and SF.

1954   "The Meaning of Western Defense."   Dissent
(Spring, 1954), 157-65.   Essay.   Reprinted
in AM.

"David Riesman Reconsidered." <u>Dissent</u> (Autumn,
1954), 349-59. Essay. Reprinted in <u>AM</u>.

1955 "The Homosexual Villain." <u>One: The Homosexual Magazine</u>, January, 1955, pp. 8-12.
Essay. Reprinted in <u>AM</u>.

"What I Think of Artistic Freedom." <u>Dissent</u>
(Spring, 1955), 98, 192-93. Essay.

1956 "Quickly." <u>Village Voice</u>, January 11 to May 2.
Weekly column.
January 11, p. 5. Reprinted in <u>AM</u>.
January 18, pp. 5, 11. Reprinted in <u>AM</u>.
January 25, p. 5. Reprinted in <u>AM</u>.
February 1, p. 5 (also letter, p. 11).
February 8, p. 5.
February 15, pp. 5, 10.
February 22, pp. 5, 14 (also letter, p. 4).
February 29, pp. 5, 9.
March 7, p. 5.
March 14, pp. 5, 9.
March 21, pp. 5, 11.
March 28, pp. 5, 11.
April 4, p. 5.
April 11, p. 5.
April 18, p. 5.
April 25, p. 5.
May 2, p. 5. Reprinted in <u>AM</u>.

1956 "A Public Notice by Norman Mailer." <u>Village
Voice</u>, May 9, 1956, p. 12. Advertisement
reviewing Beckett's <u>Waiting for Godot</u>. Reprinted in <u>AM</u>.

"The Tragedy of Parris Island." <u>Dissent</u> (Fall,
1956), 435. Essay.

"The Man Who Studied Yoga." <u>New Short Novels
II</u>. New York: Ballantine, 1956, pp. 1-29.
Novella. Reprinted in AM and SF.

1957 "The White Negro: Superficial Reflections on the

Hipster." Dissent (Summer, 1957), 276-93. Essay. Reprinted in AM and as paperback. See "Primary Sources: Books."

1958 "Reflections on Hipsterism." Dissent (Winter, 1958), 73-81. Essay. Reprinted as "Reflections on Hip" in AM.

"Advertisements for Myself on the Way Out." Partisan Review (Fall, 1958), 519-40. Story. Reprinted in AM with subtitle: "Prologue to a long novel."

"The Captain" [section from A Calculus at Heaven]. Artesian [Ann Arbor, Michigan], 4 (Winter, 1958-59), 9-16.

1959 "Comment." Dissent (Winter, 1959), pp. 9-10. On "A New Political Atmosphere in America" by Irving Howe. Reprinted in AM.

"From Surplus Value to Mass Media." Dissent (Summer, 1959), 254-57. Essay. Reprinted in AM.

"Buddies or the Hole in the Summit, An Apocryphal and Interrupted Transcript." Village Voice, September 16, 1959, pp. 1, 4-5. One-act play. Reprinted without subtitle in AM.

"Scenes from The Deer Park." Partisan Review (Fall, 1959), 527-34. Play. Reprinted in AM.

"The Mind of an Outlaw." Esquire, November, 1959, pp. 87-94. Essay. Reprinted in AM.

"An Eye on Picasso." Provincetown Annual, 1959, pp. 27-28. Essay. Reprinted in AM.

1960 "The Shining Enemies." Nation, January 30, 1960, inside cover. Letter in response to Gore Vidal's review of AM.

"A Program for the Nation." <u>Dissent</u> (Winter, 1960), 67-70. Essay. Reprinted in <u>PP</u>.

"She Thought the Russians Was Coming." <u>Esquire</u>, June, 1960, pp. 129-34. Essay. Reprinted in <u>Dissent</u> (Summer, 1961), 408-12 and in <u>PP</u>.

"Superman Comes to the Supermart." <u>Esquire</u>, November, 1960, pp. 119-29. Essay. Reprinted as "Superman Comes to the Supermarket" in <u>PP</u> and <u>IO</u>.

1961   Letter to the Editor. <u>Esquire</u>, January, 1961, p. 15. Letter.

"An Open Letter to JFK and Fidel Castro." <u>Village Voice</u>, April 27, 1961, pp. 1, 14-15. Letters. Reprinted in <u>PP</u>.

"The Blacks." <u>Village Voice</u>, May 11, 1961, pp. 11, 14 (Part I); May 18, 1961, pp. 11, 14-15 (Part II). Essay. Reprinted in <u>PP</u>.

"Mailer to Hansberry." <u>Village Voice</u>, June 8, 1961, pp. 11-12. Letter.

"Sex and Censorship in Literature and the Arts." <u>Playboy</u>, July, 1961, pp. 27-28, 72, 74, 76, 88, 92, 95-99. Discussion contribution. Partially reprinted as part of "Petty Notes on Some Sex in America" in <u>CC</u>.

"The First Day's Interview." <u>Paris Review</u>, 26 (Summer-Fall, 1961), 140-53. Self-interview. Reprinted in abridged form in <u>CC</u>.

"Gourmandise." <u>New Yorker</u>, September 16, 1961, p. 107. Poem. Reprinted in <u>DL</u>.

"To the Lower Classes." <u>New Statesman</u> (September 29, 1961), 445. Poem.

"Eternities." New Yorker, November 11, 1961,
   p. 200. Poem. Reprinted in DL.

"Open Poem to John Fitzgerald Kennedy."
   Village Voice, November 23, 1961, p. 4.
   Poem. Reprinted in Dissent (Winter, 1962),
   33-34 and in PP and IO.

"Foreword" to Views of a Nearsighted Cannoneer
   by Seymour Krim. New York: Excelsior,
   1961, p. [6]. One paragraph.

1962 "Poems." Atlantic, January, 1962, p. 62.
   Poems. Reprinted in DL.

"A Glass of Milk." Village Voice, February 1,
   1962, p. 4. Poem. Reprinted in PP.

"Poem to the Book Review at Time." Time,
   April 6, 1962, p. 12. Poem-letter in response to Time's review of DL. Reprinted
   in PP.

"The Womanization of America." Playboy, June,
   1962, pp. 43-50, 133-34, 136, 139-44. Discussion contribution. Partially reprinted in
   IO and as part of "Petty Notes on Some Sex
   in America" in CC.

"An Evening with Jackie Kennedy." Esquire,
   July, 1962, pp. 56-61. Essay. Reprinted
   as "The Existential Heroine" in PP and IO.

"Truth and Being: Nothing and Time." Evergreen Review, September-October, 1962,
   pp. 68-74. Story. Reprinted with subtitle:
   "A Broken Fragment from a Long Novel" in
   PP, SF and in Evergreen Review Reader, ed.
   Barney Rosset. New York: Castle Books,
   1968, pp. 468-70.

"The Big Bite." Esquire, November, 1962,

p. 134; December, 1962, p. 168.   Monthly
column continued throughout 1963.   Partially
reprinted in PP.

"Responses and Reactions I." Commentary (December, 1962), 504-06.   First column in a
series.   Partially reprinted in PP.

"Open Letter to JFK." Village Voice, December 20, 1962, pp. 1, 7.   Reprinted in PP
and partially reprinted in IO.

"Sing the Ballad of the Sad Saint." Esquire,
December, 1962, p. 169.   Poem.   Reprinted
in PP and as "The Ride of the Sad Saint" in
CC.

1963   "Punching Papa." New York Review of Books,
Special Issue, Winter, 1963, p. 13.   Review
of That Summer in Paris by Morley Callaghan.
Reprinted in CC.

Untitled.   ["One never hears the words intended
...].   Way Out [Journal of The School of
Living, Brookville, Ohio], January, 1963,
p. 20.   Poem.

"Two Poems: 'Smog doggerel for the haze' and
'Static'." Way Out, February, 1963, p. 49.

"The Big Bite." Esquire, November, 1962 to
December, 1963.   Monthly column.
January, p. 65.   Partially reprinted in PP.
February, pp. 109-21.   Reprinted as "Ten
Thousand Words a Minute" in PP.
March, pp. 98, 138.   Partially reprinted in
PP; reprinted in IO.
April, p. 74.   Partially reprinted in PP;
reprinted in IO.
May, pp. 37, 40.   Partially reprinted in PP.
June, pp. 23, 24, 28, 32.   Reprinted in CC.
July, pp. 63-69, 105.   Titled "Some Children
of the Goddess" and reprinted in CC.

August, pp. 16-24. Reprinted in PP.

September, pp. 16-20. Partially reprinted
in CC.

October, pp. 50-52. First half reprinted in PP
and partially in November, 1963. "Big Bite."
Second half reprinted as "Two Oddments from
Esquire" in EE.

November, pp. 26-32. Partially reprinted in PP.

December, pp. 22-26.

"The Real Meaning of the Right Wing in America."
Playboy, January, 1963, pp. 111-12, 165,
167-70, 172-74. Essay. (Subtitled "Opposing
Statements on the Role of the Right Wing in
America Today: A Liberal's View" by Play-
boy). Reprinted in PP and IO.

Letter to the Editor. Playboy, February, 1963,
p. 15. Letter protesting being labelled
"liberal" in subtitle above.

"The Role of the Right Wing." Playboy,
February, 1963, pp. 115-16, 119-22. Debate with William F. Buckley, Jr.

"Responses and Reactions." Commentary, semi-
monthly column.
December, 1962 to October, 1963.
February, pp. 146-48. Reprinted in PP.
April, pp. 335-37. Reprinted in PP.
June, pp. 517-58. Reprinted in PP.
August, pp. 164-65. Reprinted in CC.
October, pp. 320-21. Reprinted in PP.

"Classes." New Statesman (February 8, 1963),
207. Poem. Reprinted in PP.

"The First Presidential Paper." Dissent (Summer, 1963), 249-54. Essay. Reprinted in
PP.

"Jean Genet and 'The Blacks'--An Impulse to
Destroy." Panorama (Chicago Daily News),

July 13, 1963, p. 3.   Essay.

"The Leading Man."   Book Week, September 29,
1963, pp. 16-17.   Review of JFK: Man and
Myth by Victor Lasky.   Reprinted in CC and
IO.

"The Mary McCarthy Case."   New York Review
of Books, October 17, 1963, pp. 1-3.   Review of The Group.   Reprinted as "The Case
Against McCarthy" in CC.

"The Fate of the Union: Kennedy and After."
New York Review of Books, December 26,
1963, p. 6.   Discussion contribution.

"The Last Night."   Esquire, December, 1963,
pp. 151, 274-80.   Story.   Reprinted in CC
and SF.

1964   "Mailer vs. Scully."   Architectural Forum,
April, 1964, pp. 96-97.   Portions of two
"Big Bite" columns with afterword.   Reprinted
in CC and IO.

"The Killer."   Evergreen Review, April-May,
1964, pp. 26+.   Story.   Reprinted in CC and
SF.

"Architects: Blindness Is the Fruit of Your De-
sign."   Village Voice, June 18, 1964, p. 5.
Essay.

An American Dream.   Novel serialized in
Esquire, January to August.   [Revised and
published as book in 1965].
January: "The Harbors of the Moon"
February: "Messenger from the Casino"
March: "A Messenger from the Maniac"
April: "Green Circles of Exhaustion"
May: "A Caternary of Manners"
June: "A Vision in the Desert"
July: "A Votive Is Prepared"

August: "At the Lion and the Serpent"

"The Executioner's Song." Fuck You, Magazine of the Arts, September, 1964, pp. [23-25]. Poem. Reprinted in CC.

"A Vote for Bobby K.--Possibility of a Hero." Village Voice, October 29, 1964, pp. 4, 10. Essay. Reprinted in CC and IO.

"My Hope for America: A Review of a Book by Lyndon B. Johnson." Book Week, November 1, 1964, pp. 1, 7-8. Essay. Reprinted in CC and IO.

"In the Red Light: A History of the Republican Convention of 1964." Esquire, November, 1964, pp. 83-89, 167. Essay. Reprinted in CC and IO.

"Special Preface" to The Presidential Papers. New York: Bantam Books, 1964.

1965 "Cities Higher than Mountains." New York Times Magazine, January 30, 1965, pp. 16-17. Essay. Reprinted in CC.

"Norman Mailer on LBJ." Realist, June, 1965, pp. 1, 10-15. Essay. Reprinted as "A Speech at Berkeley on Vietnam Day" in CC and IO.

"On Vietnam." Partisan Review (Fall, 1965), pp. 638-39, 641-43, 645-46. Essay. Reprinted in CC and partially in IO.

"Norman Mailer on Lindsay and the City." Village Voice, October 28, 1965, p. 1. Essay. Reprinted in CC and IO.

1966 "3--Poems." East Side Review, January-February, 1966, p. 43. Poems. Reprinted in CC.

"Modes and Mutations: Comments on the Modern
American Novel." Commentary, March, 1966,
pp. 37-40. Essay. Reprinted in CC.

Letter to the Editor. New York Review of Books,
April 28, 1966, pp. 26-27. Letter answering
Richard Stern's article on Mailer at the 1965
MLA. Reprinted in EE.

"On Cannibals and Christians." Dissent (May-
June, 1966), 304-06. Essay. Reprinted as
"On Introducing Our Argument" in CC.

"Rush to Judgment." Village Voice, September 1,
1966, pp. 1, 24-27. Review of book by Mark
Lane. Reprinted in EE. Published as "The
Great American Mystery" in Book Week,
August 28, 1966, pp. 1, 11-13.

"The Writer and Hollywood." Film Heritage, 2
(Fall, 1966), 23. Two paragraphs answering
editor's questions.

"Henry Miller," in Double Exposure by Roddy
McDowell. New York: Delacorte, 1966,
pp. 168-69. Biographical sketch. Reprinted
in EE.

1967 "A Requiem for the Rube." Village Voice,
January 5, 1967, pp. 4, 16. Essay.

"A Statement of Aims." Village Voice,
January 5, 1967, p. 16. On The Deer Park
play.

"In Clay's Corner." Partisan Review (Summer,
1967), 461. Statement on Cassius Clay's draft
status.

"Mr. Mailer Interviews Himself." New York
Times Book Review, September 17, 1967,
pp. 4-5, 40. Self-interview. Reprinted as
"An Imaginary Interview" in EE.

"The Crazy One." Playboy, October, 1967,
pp. 91-92, 112, 211-14. Essay. Reprinted
as "Footnote to Death in the Afternoon" in
The Bullfight: A Photographic Narrative with
Text by Norman Mailer and as "Homage to
El Loco" in EE.

García Lorca, Federico. "Lament for Ignatio
Sanchez Mejías." Trans. by Susan and Norman Mailer in The Bullfight. (Read by
Mailer on phonograph record available with
The Bullfight.) Reprinted in The Poetry Bag,
ed. R. P. Dickey, et al. Columbia, Mis-
souri: 1967, pp. 5-10 and as "A Translation
from Lorca" in EE.

"The Playwright as Critic." Introduction to The
Deer Park: A Play. Reprinted in EE.

"Some Dirt in the Talk: A Candid History of an
Existential Movie Called Wild 90." Esquire,
December, 1967, pp. 190-98, 261. Re-
printed in EE.

1968 "The Steps of the Pentagon." Harper's, March,
1968, pp. 47-142. Reprinted as part of
The Armies of the Night.

"The Battle of the Pentagon." Commentary,
April, 1968, pp. 33-37. Reprinted as part
of The Armies of the Night.

"Up the Family Tree." Partisan Review (Spring,
1968), 235-52. Essay-review of Making It by
Norman Podhoretz. Reprinted in EE.

"Black Power: A Discussion." Partisan Review
(Spring, 1968), 218-21. Symposium contribution. Reprinted in EE.

[Untitled]. Partisan Review (Summer, 1968), 490.
Reply to Irving Howe's comments on the Black
Power Symposium.

[Untitled]. Partisan Review (Fall, 1968), 649-
50. Continued exchange with Howe.

"Miami Beach and Chicago." Harper's, November, 1968, pp. 41-52, 55-56, 69-84, 89-104,
107-30. Revised as Miami and the Siege of
Chicago.

"An Open Letter to Richard Nixon." Newsweek,
December 9, 1968, p. 85. Reprinted in EE.

Introduction to The Idol and the Octopus.

[Note: Mailer also wrote a preface to The Saint
and the Psychopath (printed in EE), a book
intended as the third in the Dell series including The Short Fiction of Norman Mailer
and The Idol and the Octopus but never published.]

1969 "Looking for the Meat and Potatoes: Thoughts on
Black Power." Look, January 7, 1969, pp.
57-60. Essay. Reprinted in EE.

"Twentieth National Book Awards." Publishers'
Weekly, March 24, 1969, pp. 26-27. National Book Award acceptance speech. Reprinted as "Accepting the National Book
Award" in EE.

"Who is to Declare That the Minority Do Not De-
serve to Determine the Schools' History?"
New York Times Magazine, May 4, 1969,
pp. 35+. Essay.

"On Accepting the Pulitzer Prize." Village Voice,
May 6, 1969, p. 5. Acceptance speech. Reprinted in RM.

"Why Are We in New York?" New York Times
Magazine, May 18, 1969, pp. 30-31+. Essay.
Reprinted in RM and as "An Instrument for
the City" in EE.

"Be My Guest, Norman Mailer." New York Post, July 1, 1969. Guest column. Reprinted in RM, pp. 138-40.

Dedication in RM, p. [v]. One-paragraph dedication dated July 22, 1969.

"A Fire on the Moon." Life, August 29, 1969, pp. 22-41. Revised for Of a Fire on the Moon.

"The Psychology of Astronauts." Life, November 14, 1969, pp. 50-63. Revised for Of a Fire on the Moon.

"Foreword" to The End of Obscenity by Charles Rembar. London: Andre Deutsch, 1969, pp. [viii]-xi. Essay. Reprinted in EE.

"Speech at the John Jay College of Criminal Justice" in RM. Text of May 6, 1969, speech.

"At the Village Gate" in RM. Text of May 7, 1969, speech. Reprinted in EE.

"Mayoral Candidates Debate, Norman Mailer and Others" in RM. Text of May 15, 1969, television debate.

"A Speech to the Time-Life Staff" in RM. Text of speech. Reprinted in EE.

1970 "A Dream of the Future's Face." Life, January 9, 1970, pp. 56-74. Revised for Of a Fire on the Moon.

Letter in This is My Best, ed. Whit Burnett. Garden City, New York: Doubleday, 1970, pp. 99-100. Letter to Whit Burnett prefacing Mailer's selection.

1971 "Ego." Life, March 19, 1971, pp. 18f, 19, 22-30, 32, 36. Reprinted as "King of the Hill" in EE and as separate paperback.

"Prisoner of Sex." Harper's, March, 1971,
pp. 41-46+. Revised as The Prisoner of
Sex.

Letter to Editor. Saturday Review, April 20,
1971. Reply to Stuart Little's "What Happened at Harper's." Reprinted in EE.

Letter to Communications Editor. Saturday Review, June 12, 1971, p. 56. Letter.

Letter to Editor. New York Times Book Review,
June 13, 1971. Letter in response to Brigid
Brophy's review of The Prisoner of Sex
(May 23). Reprinted in EE.

"Preface" to Sting Like a Bee: The Muhammad
Ali Story by José Torres. New York:
Curtis Books, 1971, pp. 5-11.

"A Course in Film-Making." New American Review #12. New York: Simon and Schuster,
1971, pp. 200-41. Reprinted in Maidstone:
A Mystery and EE.

1972 "The Evil in the Room." Life, July 28, 1972,
pp. 26-33, 36-41. Revised for St. George
and the Godfather.

"The Genius." New York Review of Books,
November 2, 1972, pp. 16-20. Revised por-
tion of St. George and the Godfather, published simultaneously with it.

1973 "The Morning After." New York Times Book
Review, March 11, 1973, pp. 55, 46. Essay
on fiftieth birthday party and Fifth Estate.

"A Transit to Narcissus: Last Tango in Paris."
New York Review of Books, May 17, 1973,
pp. 3-10. Essay. Reprinted in Bernardo

Bertolucci's Last Tango in Paris: The
Screenplay. New York: Dell, 1974.

"An Open Letter to the Members of the Com-
munist Party of the Soviet Union." New
York Review of Books, June 28, 1973, p. 7.
Letter signed (but not written) by Mailer and
twenty-one others.

"Marilyn." Ladies' Home Journal, July, 1973,
pp. 79-83, 106, 108, 110-11 and August,
1973, pp. 79, 126-28, 130-34. Excerpts
from Marilyn: A Novel Biography.

"The Jewish Princess." Atlantic, August, 1973,
pp. 33-53. Excerpt from Marilyn.

"Married to Marilyn." New York Review of
Books, August 9, 1973, pp. 11-14. Excerpt
from Marilyn.

1974 "The Faith of Graffiti." Esquire, May, 1974,
pp. 77-88, 154, 157-58. Excerpt from The
Faith of Graffiti with photographs by Jon
Naar.

"The Talk of the Town." New Yorker, May 20,
1974, p. 34. Comments on Nixon tapes.

Introduction to The Joker by Jean Malaquais.
New York: Warner, 1974.

"Expletive Restored." Village Voice, June 14-
21, 1974, p. 4. A three-paragraph
parody of presidential tapes.

C.   SELECTED EXCERPTS AND ANTHOLOGIZATIONS

NOTE: Mailer's work has been so widely anthologized that I could not locate all possible citations.   What follows are those I have found.

Excerpts from: The Naked and the Dead, Barbary Shore, The Deer Park, The Deer Park: A Play, Advertisements for Myself, Deaths for the Ladies and other disasters, The Presidential Papers, An American Dream, Cannibals and Christians, Why Are We in Vietnam?, The Armies of the Night, Miami and the Siege of Chicago, and Of a Fire on the Moon:

Lucid, Robert F. , ed.   The Long Patrol: 25 Years of Writing from the Work of Norman Mailer.   New York: World, 1971.   739 pages with general introduction and introductions to each excerpt.

The Naked and the Dead

Gould, James A. and John J. Iorio, eds.   "I Hate Everything Which is Not in Myself" in Violence in Modern Literature.   San Francisco: Boyd and Fraser, 1972, pp. 133-141.

Advertisements for Myself

Culler, Jonathan D. , ed.   "Maybe Next Year" in Harvard Advocate Centennial Anthology.   Cambridge: Schenkman, 1966, pp. 258-62.

Ferguson, Mary Anne, ed. "The Time of Her Time" in Images of Women in Literature. Boston: Houghton Mifflin, 1973, pp. 280-99.

Gross, Barry, ed. "The White Negro" in For Our Time: 24 Essays by 8 Contemporary Americans. New York: Dodd, Mead, 1970. [Also includes excerpts from Cannibals and Christians and The Armies of the Night.]

Hersey, John, ed. "The Last Draft of The Deer Park" in The Writer's Craft. New York: Knopf, 1974, pp. 343-61.

McMichael, George, et al., eds. "The White Negro," "The Man Who Studied Yoga," "Sixth Advertisement for Myself" in Anthology of American Literature, Vol. II: Realism to the Present. New York: Macmillan, 1974, pp. 1826-74.

Schorer, Mark, ed. "The White Negro" in The Literature of America: Twentieth Century. New York: McGraw-Hill, 1970, pp. 1094-1111.

"The Taming of Denise Gondelman" in Avant Garde, I (May, 1968), 41-45 ["The Time of Her Time" with first section omitted].

The Presidential Papers

Gross, Theodore L., ed. "The Existential Hero: Superman Comes to the Supermarket" in Representative Men: Cult Heroes of Our Time. New York: Free Press, 1970, pp. 6-12.

Rosset, Barney, ed. "Truth and Being: Nothing and Time: a broken fragment from a long novel" in Evergreen Review Reader. New York: Castle Books, 1968, pp. 468-70.

Cannibals and Christians

Gross, Barry, ed. "Cities Higher Than Mountains" in
   For Our Time: 24 Essays by 8 Contemporary
   Americans. New York: Dodd, Mead, 1970.
   [Also includes excerpts from Advertisements for
   Myself and The Armies of the Night.]

Klein, Marcus, ed. "The Argument Reinvigorated"
   (MLA Address) in The American Novel Since
   World War II. New York: Fawcett, 1969,
   pp. 69-77.

The Armies of the Night

Bradley, et al., eds. "Justice," "A Confrontation by
   the River," "Bust 80: Beyond the Law" in The
   American Tradition in Literature, Vol. 2, Fourth
   Edition. New York: Norton, 1974.

Brooks, Lewis, and Warren, eds. "2: The Marshal
   and the Nazi" and "3: Grandma with Orange
   Hair" in American Literature: The Makers and
   the Making, Vol. II. New York: St. Martin's
   Press, 1973, pp. 2883-90.

Gross, Barry, ed. "The Battle of the Pentagon" in
   For Our Time: 24 Essays by 8 Contemporary
   Americans. New York: Dodd, Mead, 1970.
   [Also includes excerpts from Advertisements for
   Myself and Cannibals and Christians.]

Wolfe, Tom and E. W. Johnson, eds. "A Confrontation by the River" and "Bust 80: Beyond the
   Law" in The New Journalism. New York: Harper & Row, 1973, pp. 188-96.

Of a Fire on the Moon

Anderson, Margaret, ed. Pp. 300-01 in Mother Was
   Not a Person. Montreal: Content Publishing.

Bellamy, Joe David, ed. Pp. 202-08 in <u>Apocalypse:</u>
    <u>Dominant Contemporary Forms</u>. New York:
    Lippincott, 1972.

Braudy, Leo. Excerpts in <u>Film Focus</u> on <u>Shoot the</u>
    <u>Piano Player</u>. Englewood Cliffs, New Jersey:
    Prentice-Hall, 1972.

Decker, Randall, ed. Pp. 36-42 in <u>Patterns of Ex-</u>
    <u>position</u>, Third Edition. Boston: Little, Brown,
    1972.

McQuade, Donald A. and Robert Atwen, eds. "The
    First Moon Walk" in <u>Popular Writing in America:</u>
    <u>The Interaction of Style and Audience</u>. New York:
    Oxford University Press, 1974, pp. 638-47.

Moffett, et al., eds. Chapter 2, pp. 28-34 in
    <u>Reportage and Research 2 (IV): Interaction</u>
    <u>Series</u>. Boston: Houghton Mifflin.

Regush, Nicholas. Pp. 44-49 in <u>Visibles and Invisibles</u>.
    Boston: Little, Brown, 1973.

Schorer, Durham, Jones, eds. Pp. 4-17 in <u>The</u>
    <u>Harbrace College Reader</u>, Fourth Edition. New
    York: Harcourt Brace Jovanovich, 1972.

Shrodes, Caroline, et al., eds. "A Burial by the Sea"
    in <u>The Conscious Reader</u>. New York: Macmillan,
    1974, pp. 766-75.

Weber, Ronald, ed. Excerpts in <u>America in Change</u>.
    South Bend: Notre Dame University Press, 1972.

White, James B. Selection from p. 25 and pp. 273-
    74 in <u>The Legal Imagination: Studies in the</u>
    <u>Nature of Legal Expression</u>. Boston: Little,
    Brown, 1973.

"King of the Hill"

McQuade, Donald A. and Robert Atwen, eds. "The
    Ali-Frazier Fight" in Popular Writing in America:
    The Interaction of Style and Audience. New York:
    Oxford University Press, 1974, pp. 365-72.

The Prisoner of Sex

Korda, Michael. Excerpts in Male Chauvinism, How It
    Works. New York: Random House, 1973.

Unidentified Excerpts

Bower, Reuben A. , ed. Twentieth Century Literature
    in Retrospect. Cambridge: Harvard University
    Press, 1971.

Conron, John H. , ed. The American Landscape: A
    Critical Anthology of Prose and Poetry. New
    York: Oxford University Press, 1974.

Gillespie, Sheena and Linda C. Stanley. Someone Like
    Me: Images for Writing. New York: Winthrop,
    1973.

Hayes, Harold. Smiling Through the Apocalypse:
    Esquire's History of the Sixties. New York:
    Delta, 1973.

Mills, Nicholaus, ed. The New Journalism: A His-
    torical Anthology. New York: McGraw-Hill,
    1974.

Porter, Roger L. The Voice Within: Reading and
    Writing Autobiography. New York: Knopf, 1973.

Sigal, Leon V. Reporters and Officials: The Organi-
    zation and Politics of Newsmaking. Lexington,
    Massachusetts: Lexington Books, 1973.

Solotaroff, Theodore, ed. Writers and Issues. New
      York: New American Library, 1972.

Tibbets, A. M. and Charlene Tibbets. The Critical
      Man. Glenview, Illinois: Scott Foresman, 1972.

D. FILMS

Note: Mailer conceived, directed, and acted in all of these films. All are distributed by New Line Cinema, 121 University Place, New York.

Wild 90, 1967
Beyond the Law - Red, 1968
Beyond the Law - Blue, 1968 [Mailer's reediting of
     Beyond the Law - Red]
Maidstone, 1970

E. PLAYS PRODUCED

The Deer Park. First produced at the Actors' Studio, New York, 1959-60. 127 performances beginning January 31, 1967 at the Theatre de Lys, New York.

D. J. Performed in Provincetown, Massachusetts during the summer of 1967. Printed as "A Fragment from Vietnam" in EE.

See also Jack Gelber's Barbary Shore in Secondary Sources, Nonprint Media.

F. UNPUBLISHED MANUSCRIPTS

1938-39

"The Collision," n. d. Story.   Probably a high school
story.

1940-43

"The Lady Wears a Smile," early February, 1940.
First story at Harvard.   Ms. also includes a
vignette: "Nice White Tablecloths. "

"Nice White Tablecloths" and "It's Only That I Love
You, " early 1940.   One page with two vignettes.

"Pick Them Up and Lay Them Down, " February 17 and
18, 1940.   Story.

"So He Wrote a Book About It, " February 29, 1940.
Classroom exercise, a review of the Studs
Lonigan Trilogy by James T. Farrell.

"Some Miss Their It, " March 11-13, 1940.   Story.

"Life Is Where You Find It, " April 4-10, 1940.   Story.

"Now I Lay Me Down to Sleep" [another copy is titled
"Prelude to Sleep"], April 20-21, 1940.   Story.

"No, Mother, " May 10, 1940.   Story.

Untitled ["Fred, Semour and I were sitting around.... "],

June 20-25, 1940. Story.

"Oh, Don't You Be That Way," June, 1940. Story.

"He Was Her Man," July 12, 1940. Story.

Untitled ["He was riding down a long, curling, rutted
    road...."], July 22, 1940. Story.

"The Source of the Grief," July, 1940. Story.

"The Principle of the Thing," August, 1940. Story.

"I'll See You in the Morning," September 19, 1940.
    Story.

"Her Eyes and Her Hair," September, 1940. Story.

"Today Is Sunday," October 25 and 27, 1940. Story.

"Beer Bottle Polka," November, 1940. Story.

"Then She Says to Salvy," December, 1940. Story.

"Me and You," February 1, 1941. Story.

"Mr. Berliner Establishes a Mile-Post," March 14,
    1941. Story.

No Percentage, June-September, 1941. First novel
    completed while at Harvard, 488 pages. Epigraph
    is a three-paragraph story beginning "He was
    creeping along next to the barbed wire...."

"Four Pamphlets for Jesus," November 7, 1941. Story.

"The Schedule Breaker," December 5, 1941. Story.

"Report on 'Soap' by James T. Farrell," December 12,
    1941. Classroom exercise. Attached is list of
    stories by Farrell and Dorothy Parker "read this
    month."

"A Clean Well-Ordered Life," late 1941.   Story.

"Retreat," February 18, 1942.   Story.

"Charde and Dana," March 2, 1942.   Story.

"Land Lashed," April 1, 1942.   Story.

"The Lock," July 17, 1942.   Story.

"Three Fingers of Friendship," 1942-43.   Story.

A Transit to Narcissus, September 1942-43.   Second
    novel completed while at Harvard, 523 pages.

Untitled ["It wasn't until the New York train was
    leaving Back Bay Station...."], February 26,
    1943.   Story.

"Allegory," n.d.   Poem.

"But What Does It Say?: A very brief analysis of The
    Sound and the Fury by William Faulkner," n.d.
    Classroom exercise.

"Duet," n.d.   Story.

"Fair Harvard, Thy Sons ...," n.d.   Story

"Good to See You," n.d.   Story.

"Harmony in Three Voices," n.d.   Story.

"Just Don't," n.d.   Story.

"Love-Buds," n.d.   Story.

"Man Overboard," n.d.   Story.

"Music Teachers I Have Known and Loved," n.d.
    Story.

"A Page of Shorts," n.d.   Three vignettes: "Rape,"
    "It Shouldn't Happen to a Dog" [published as "It"
    in Advertisements for Myself], "Double-Talk."

[The Naked and the Dead, summer, 1943.   Play about
    insane asylum.   Not in vault.]

                          1944-47

Untitled ["Something rather terrible happened last
    night...."], n.d., post-1944.   War story.

"The Smile of Recognition," n.d., post-1944.   War
    story.

"Nostalgia," January and February, 1945.   Story
    written in Luzon.

"Dr. Bulfanoff and the Solitary Teste," n.d., post-war.
    Story.

                          1948-50

"A Note on the '48 Election," n.d., 1948.   Short essay.

Character of the Victim by Jean Malaquais and Norman
    Mailer, 102 pages and "A Note on Peter and
    Victor," ix pages, n.d., late 1949 or early 1950.
    Movie treatment.

Our Different Lives: Stories by Norman Mailer, Jean
    Malaquais, Louis Zara, n.d., late 1949 or early
    1950.   Movie treatment.   Four stories including
    "The Greatest Thing in the World" and a section
    on Minetta from The Naked and the Dead.

                          1954-56

"Notebook for Bullfighting Book," July 22-October 10,
    1954.   Notebook containing paragraphs numbered
    1 to 73 on impressions of bullfighting.

The Deer Park, 1954, 247 pages.   Original Rinehart
     version of the novel in cut galleys.

Pen Club Speech, 1955.   Text of speech.

1960-67

"A Letter from Provincetown," June 29, 1960.   Reply
     to New York Post story on the Provincetown in-
     cident of June 9, 1960 when Mailer was arrested
     for being drunk and disorderly.   [Submitted to
     New York Post and Village Voice.   May have
     been published.]

A fragment of an essay on the death of Camus, October,
     1960-February, 1961.

Interview with Richard Poirier, early 1966.

Essay of nine pages on the genesis of The Deer Park:
     A Play, 1967.

II.   SECONDARY SOURCES

A.   REVIEWS AND ARTICLES
ON SPECIFIC BOOKS

The Naked and the Dead (1948)

Burg, David F.   "The Hero of The Naked and the
Dead," Modern Fiction Studies, 17 (Autumn,
1971), 387-401.

Coan, Otis and Richard G. Lillard.   America in Fiction, 5th ed.   Palo Alto, California: Pacific
Books, 1967, p. 126.

Dedman, Emmett.   Chicago Sun, May 9, 1948, p. 8x.

Dempsey, David.   New York Times, May 9, 1948,
p. 6.

Eisinger, Chester E.   "The American War Novel: An
Affirming Flame."   Pacific Spectator, 9 (Summer, 1955), 272-87.

_____.   Fiction of the Forties.   Chicago: University
of Chicago Press, 1963, pp. 33-38, 93-94 et
passim.

_____.   "Introduction" in The Naked and the Dead.
New York: Holt, Rinehart and Winston, 1968,
pp. vii-xxv.

Enkvist, Nils Erik.   "Re-readings: Norman Mailer,

The Naked and the Dead." Moderna Språk, 56
(1962), 60-64.

Farrelly, John. "Fiction Parade." New Republic,
May 17, 1948, p. 32.

Foley, Martha. Survey G, 37 (December, 1948), 499.

Frederick, John T. "Fiction of the Second World War."
College English, 17 (January, 1956), 197-204.

Geismar, Maxwell. "Nightmare on Anopopei."
Saturday Review, January 8, 1949, pp. 10-11.
Reprinted in America Moderns: From Rebellion
to Conformity. New York: Hill and Wang, 1958,
pp. 171-73.

Gordon, Andrew. "The Naked and the Dead: The
Triumph of Impotence." Literature and Psychology, 19 (1969), 3-13.

Humboldt, Charles. Masses and Mainstream, August,
1948, p. 70.

Kahm, Lothar. "The Jewish Soldier in Modern Fiction." American Judaism, 9 (1960), 12-13, 30-
31.

Kalem, Theodore. Christian Science Monitor, September 16, 1948, p. 11.

Kirkus, 16 (March 1, 1948), 126.

Lardner, John. "Pacific Battle, Good and Big." New
Yorker, May 15, 1948, pp. 115-17.

Lutwack, Leonard. Heroic Fiction: The Epic Tradition
and American Novels of the Twentieth Century.
Carbondale: Southern Illinois University Press,
1971.

Match, Richard. "Souls of Men Stripped by Battle and
Boredom." New York Herald Tribune Book

Review, May 9, 1948, p. 3.

Maurois, André.   "La Guerre, Jugeé par un Romancier Americain."   Nouvelles Litteraires, August 27, 1950, p. 5.

"Men in War."   Newsweek, May 10, 1948, pp. 86-87.

New York Times, May 7, 1948, p. 21;   December 20, 1948, p. 23.

"No British Action against Naked and the Dead."   Publishers' Weekly, 155 (June 4, 1949), 2300.

Prescott, Orville.   "Outstanding Novels."   Yale Review, 37 (Summer, 1948), 765.

Publishers' Weekly, 155 (January 22, 1949), 270.

Rideout, Walter B.   The Radical Novel in the United States: 1900-1954.   Cambridge: Harvard University Press, 1956, pp. 270-73.

Rolo, Charles J.   "Reader's Choice."   Atlantic, June, 1948, p. 114.

Rosenthal, Raymond.   Commentary, July, 1948, p. 92.

"Rugged Times."   New Yorker, October 23, 1948, p. 25.

Sakamoto, Masayuki.   Studies of American Novels: Norman Mailer Number (Japan), 1 (May 25, 1973).

Smith, Harrison.   Saturday Review, February 12, 1949, p. 9.

Squires, Russell.   San Francisco Chronicle.   May 23, 1948, p. 21.

Waldmeir, Joseph J.   American Novels of the Second World War.   The Hague: Mouton, 1969, pp. 15-152 passim.

Waldron, Randall H.   "The Naked, the Dead, and the
     Machine: A New Look at Norman Mailer's First
     Novel."   PMLA (March, 1972), 271-77.

"War and No Peace."   Time, May 10, 1948, pp. 106-
     109.

Wasson, Donald.   Library Journal, 73 (May 1, 1948),
     707.

Wolfert, Ira.   "War Novelist."   Nation, 166 (June 26,
     1948), 722.

Wood, G. L.   Canadian Forum, July, 1948, p. 93.

                    Barbary Shore (1951)

Cecil, L. Moffitt.   "The Passing of Arthur in Norman
     Mailer's Barbary Shore."   Research Studies of
     Washington State University, 39 (March, 1951),
     54-58.

Cogley, John.   "Books."   Commonweal, 54 (June 8,
     1951), 220-21.

Fuller, Edmund.   Chicago Sunday Tribune, May 27,
     1951, p. 4.

Geismar, Maxwell.   "Frustration, Neuroses and His-
     tory."   Saturday Review, May 26, 1951, pp. 15-
     16.   Reprinted in American Moderns: From Re-
     bellion to Conformity. New York: Hill and Wang,
     1958, pp. 173-74.

Howe, Irving.   "Some Political Novels."   Nation, 172
     (June 16, 1951), 568.   Reprinted in A World More
     Attractive. New York: Horizon Press, 1963,
     pp. 90-91.

Kirkus, 19 (March 15, 1951), 164.

"Last of the Leftists?" Time, May 28, 1951, p. 110.

McDonough, Roger H. "Fiction." Library Journal,
    76 (May 15, 1951), 862.

Match, Richard. "Mr. Mailer in the Post-war World."
    New York Herald Tribune Book Review, May 27,
    1951, p. 5.

"Other Books." Newsweek, May 28, 1951, p. 95.

Rogers, L. J. Canadian Forum, October, 1951,
    p. 167.

Rolo, Charles J. "A House in Brooklyn." Atlantic,
    June, 1951, pp. 220-21.

Stark, John. "Barbary Shore: The Basis of Mailer's
    Best Work." Modern Fiction Studies, 17
    (Autumn, 1971), 463-70.

Swados, Harvey. "Fiction Parade." New Republic,
    June 18, 1951, pp. 20-21.

Sylvester, Harry. New York Times, May 27, 1951,
    p. 5.

Vogler, Lewis. San Francisco Chronicle, June 3,
    1951, p. 11.

West, Anthony. "East Meets West, Author Meets
    Allegory." New Yorker, June 9, 1951, pp. 91-
    94.

The Deer Park [novel] (1955)

Alexander, Sidney. "Not Even Good Pornography."
    Reporter, October 20, 1955, pp. 46-48.

Alpert, Hollis. "Hollywood Saturnalia." Saturday
    Review, October 15, 1955, p. 15.

Balakian, Nona. "The Prophetic Vogue of the Anti-
    heroine." Southwest Review, 47 (Spring, 1962),
    134-41.

Bittner, William. "The Literary Underground." Nation (September 22, 1956), 247-48.

Bresler, Riva T. "Fiction." Library Journal, 80 (October 1, 1955), 2162-63.

Brooks, John. New York Times, October 16, 1955, p. 5.

Chase, Richard. "Novelist Going Places." Commentary, 20 (December, 1955), 581-83.

Cowley, Malcolm. "Mr. Mailer Tells a Tale of Love, Art, Corruption." New York Herald Tribune Book Review, October 23, 1955, p. 5.

Fitch, Robert E. "The Bourgeois and the Bohemian." Antioch Review, 16 (Summer, 1956), 135-45.

Geismar, Maxwell. "Norman Mailer: The Bohemian of National Letters" in American Moderns: From Rebellion to Conformity. New York: Hill and Wang, 1958, pp. 175-79.

Gill, Brendan. "Small Trumpet." New Yorker, October 25, 1955, pp. 161-62, 165.

Hogan, William. San Francisco Chronicle, October 13, 1955, p. 23.

Hope, F. New Statesman (April 4, 1969), 485.

Iwamoto, Iwao. Studies of American Novels: Norman Mailer Number (Japan), 1 (May 25, 1973).

Kiley, Frederick S. "Bargain Books." Clearing House, 35 (February, 1961), 379.

Kirkus, 23 (August 15, 1955), 610.

Loomis, Edward. Arizona Quarterly, 12 (Winter, 1956), 362-65.

"Love Among the Love-buckets." Time, October 17, 1955, pp. 122, 124.

New York Times, October 14, 1955, p. 25.

Nichols, Dudley. "Secret Places of the Groin." Nation, 181 (December 5, 1955), 393-95.

Pfaff, William. "The Writer as Vengeful Moralist." Commonweal, 63 (December 2, 1955), 230.

Rainer, Dachine. "Fattening for the Slaughter." New Republic, 133 (October 31, 1955), 25.

Rolo, Charles J. "The Sex Haunted Wasteland." Atlantic, November, 1955, pp. 97-98.

Spatz, Jonas. Hollywood in Fiction: Some Versions of the American Myth. The Hague: Mouton, 1969, pp. 67-132 passim.

The White Negro (1957)

No citations.

Advertisements for Myself (1959)

Baldwin, James. "The Black Boy Looks at the White Boy." Esquire, May, 1961, pp. 102-06. Reprinted in Nobody Knows My Name. New York: Dell, 1961, pp. 171-90; in Norman Mailer: A Collection of Critical Essays, ed. Leo Braudy. Englewood Cliffs, New Jersey: Prentice-Hall, 1972, pp. 66-81; and in Norman Mailer: The Man and His Work, ed. Robert F. Lucid. Boston: Little, Brown, 1971, pp. 218-237.

Bone, Robert A. "Private Mailer Re-enlists." Dissent, 7 (Autumn, 1960), 389-94.

Breslow, Paul. "The Hipster and the Radical."
    Studies on the Left, 1 (Spring, 1960), 102-05.

"Briefly Noted." New Yorker, November 14, 1959,
    pp. 233-34.

Busch, Frederick. "The Whale as Shaggy Dog: Mel-
    ville and 'The Man Who Studied Yoga'." Modern
    Fiction Studies, 19 (Summer, 1973), 193-206.

"The Crack-up." Time, November 2, 1959, p. 90.

Curley, Thomas F. "The Quarrel with Time in Amer-
    ican Fiction." American Scholar, 39 (Autumn,
    1960), 552, 554, 556, 558, 560.

DeMott, Benjamin. "Reading They've Liked." Hudson
    Review, 13 (Spring, 1960), 143-48.

Dupée, F. W. "The American Norman Mailer." Com-
    mentary, 29 (February, 1960), 128-32. Reprinted
    in Norman Mailer: A Collection of Critical Es-
    says, ed. Leo Braudy. Englewood Cliffs, New
    Jersey: Prentice-Hall, 1972, pp. 96-103.

Fiedler, Leslie A. "Antic Mailer--Portrait of a
    Middle-aged Artist." New Leader, June 25,
    1960, pp. 23-24. Reprinted in The Collected
    Essays of Leslie Fiedler. New York: Stein
    and Day, 1971, pp. 124-27.

_____. Midstream, (Winter, 1960), 100.

Finn, James. "The Virtues, Failures and Triumphs of
    an American Writer." Commonweal, 71 (Feb-
    ruary 12, 1960), 551-52.

Fleischer, L. Publishers' Weekly, 189 (January 17,
    1966), 136.

Flood, Charles B. Renascence, (Autumn, 1960), 47.

Fuller, Edmund. "Author Thinking Out Loud." New

York Herald Tribune Book Review, November 23, 1959, p. 17. Reprinted in Man in Modern Fiction: Some Minority Opinions on Contemporary American Writing. New York: Random House, 1958, pp. 154-62.

Glicksberg, Charles I. "Norman Mailer: The Angry Young Novelist in America." Wisconsin Studies in Contemporary Literature, 1 (Winter, 1960), 25-34.

Hampshire, Stuart. "Mailer United." New Statesman, October 13, 1961, pp. 515-16.

Hastings, Michael. Time and Tide (October 12, 1961), 1704.

Hicks, Granville. "The Vision of Life is His Own." Saturday Review, November 7, 1959, p. 18. Reprinted in Literary Horizons: A Quarter Century of American Fiction. New York: New York University Press, 1970, pp. 275-78.

Hoffa, W. "Norman Mailer: Advertisements for Myself" in The Fifties: Fiction, Poetry, Drama, ed. Warren G. French. Leland, Florida: Everett/Edwards, 1971, pp. 73-82.

Hogan, William. San Francisco Chronicle, November 2, 1959, p. 45; November 3, 1959, p. 35.

Horchler, Richard. Commonweal, 71 (December 4, 1959), 296.

Howe, Irving. "Mass Society and Post-modern Fiction." Partisan Review (Summer, 1959), 420-36.

_____. "A Quest for Peril." Partisan Review, 27 (Winter, 1960), 143-48.

Kazin, Alfred. "How Good Is Norman Mailer?" Reporter, November 26, 1959, pp. 40-41. Reprinted in Contemporaries. Boston: Little,

Brown, 1962, pp. 246-50 and in Norman Mailer:
the Man and His Work, ed. Robert F. Lucid.
Boston: Little, Brown, 1971, pp. 89-95.

Kiley, Frederick S.   Clearing House (February, 1961),
p. 379.

Kirkus, 27 (September 1, 1959), 667.

Krim, Seymour.   "A Hungry Mental Lion."   Evergreen
Review, 11 (January-February, 1960), 178-85.

Leverett, Ernest.   "The Virtues of Vulgarity--Russian
and American Views."   The Carleton Miscellany,
1 (Spring, 1960), 29-40.

Moore, Harry T.   "The Targets are Square."   New
York Times Book Review, November 1, 1959,
p. 4.

New York Times, November 3, 1959, p. 29.

Nyren, Karl.   "Literature."   Library Journal, 84
(September 15, 1959), 2642-43.

Petersen, Clarence.   Books Today, March 6, 1960,
p. 14.

[Review of New Short Novels, II, including "The Man
Who Studied Yoga"].   New York Times, April 29,
1956, p. 4.

Richler, Mordecai.   "Cat in the Ring."   Spectator,
207 (October 13, 1961), 510.

Rolo, Charles.   "Reader's Choice."   Atlantic, December, 1959, pp. 166-68.

Ross, Theodore J.   Chicago Jewish Forum, 20 (Fall,
1959), 57.

Sigal, Clancy.   "The Listener's Book Chronicle."   The
Listener, 66 (November 2, 1961), 738-39.

Steiner, George.   "Naked but Not Dead. "   Encounter,
    December, 1961, pp. 67-70.

"Still Promising. "   Times Literary Supplement
    (October 20, 1961), 754.

Swados, Harvey.   "Must Writers be Characters?"
    Saturday Review, October 1, 1960, pp. 12-14, 50.

Vidal, Gore.   "The Norman Mailer Syndrome."   Na-
    tion, 190 (January 2, 1960), 13-16.   Reprinted
    as "Norman Mailer's Self-Advertisements" in
    Homage to Daniel Shays: Collected Essays 1952-
    1972.   New York: Random House, 1972, pp. 75-
    86;   and as "Norman Mailer: The Angels Are
    White" in Rocking the Boat.   Boston: Little,
    Brown, 1962;   and in Norman Mailer: The Man
    and His Work, ed. Robert F. Lucid.   Boston:
    Little, Brown, 1971, pp. 95-107.

"What Might Have Been. "   Newsweek, November 9,
    1959, pp. 126-27.

Deaths for the Ladies and other disasters (1962)

Daniel, John.   Guardian, October 12, 1962, p. 9.

Dickinson, Peter.   Punch, January 2, 1962, p. 31.

Fitts, Dudley.   "Ear and Inner Eye of the Muse. "
    Saturday Review, August 4, 1962, p. 22.

Gross, John.   "Small Ads for Myself. "   New States-
    man, 64 (December 7, 1962), 830.

Hogan, William.   San Francisco Chronicle, March 28,
    1962, p. 39.

Kenner, Hugh.   "Books in Brief. "   National Review,
    13 (September 11, 1962), 200.

Macdonald, Dwight.   "Art, Life, and Violence. "

44   Norman Mailer

Commentary, August, 1962, pp. 169-72.

Palmer, David. "Poetry." Library Journal, 87
(August, 1962), 2764.

Richler, Mordecai. "Black Jacket." Spectator, 209
(October 26, 1962), 648.

Rodman, Selden. "Fast Footwork, Low Blows, and
Beating the Reader to the Punch." New York
Times Book Review, July 8, 1962, p. 7.

Ross, Alan. London Magazine, December, 1962, p. 83.

Simon, John. "More Brass than Enduring." Hudson
Review, 15 (Autumn, 1962), 457.

Swenson, May. Poetry (Chicago), May, 1962, p. 118.

Time, March 30, 1962, p. 84.

"Two Bucks--20 Dances." Newsweek, March 12, 1962,
p. 104.

The Presidential Papers (1963)

Adams, Phoebe. "Reader's Choice." Atlantic, December, 1963, pp. 164, 166.

Burns, Richard K. "Literature." Library Journal,
88 (December 1, 1963), 4645.

Capouya, Emile. "The Move Toward Immobility."
Saturday Review, November 16, 1963, pp. 37-
38, 92.

Decter, Midge. "Mailer's Campaign." Commentary,
February, 1964, pp. 83-85. Reprinted in
Norman Mailer: The Man and His Work, ed.
Robert F. Lucid. Boston: Little, Brown, 1971,
pp. 137-44 and as "Norman Mailer's Campaign"
in The Liberated Woman and Other Americans.

New York: Coward, 1971, pp. 209-15.

DeMott, Benjamin. "Conscientious Objectors?" Harper's, December, 1963, p. 110.

Galbraith, John Kenneth. "The Kennedys Didn't Reply." New York Times Book Review, November 17, 1963, p. 6.

Gilman, Richard. "Why Mailer Wants to be President." New Republic, February 8, 1964, pp. 17-20, 22-24.

Kluger, Richard. "To Dig, Get Off the Middleground." Book Week, November 10, 1963, pp. 4, 21.

"Mailer to JFK." Newsweek, November 11, 1963, pp. 110-13.

Miller, Jonathan. "Black-Mailer." Partisan Review, 31 (Winter, 1964), 103-07.

Miller, Karl. New Statesman, 67 (May 1, 1964), 690.

"Misshapen Image." Time, November 29, 1963, pp. 106, 108.

Petersen, Clarence. Books Today, February 28, 1965, p. 13.

Sigal, Clancy. "The Mailer Problem." Spectator, 7088 (May 1, 1964), 598.

Times Literary Supplement, April 30, 1964, p. 368.

"Two-edged Art of the Political Essay." Esquire, November, 1960, pp. 75-76.

Velde, Paul. "The Hemingway Who Stayed Home." Nation, 198 (January 20, 1964), 76-77.

Wills, Garry. "The Art of Not Writing Novels." National Review, 16 (January 14, 1964), 31-33.

An American Dream (1965)

Aldridge, John W. "The Big Comeback of Norman
Mailer." Life, March 19, 1965, p. 12.

Alvarez, A. "Norman X." Spectator, 7146 (May 7,
1965), 603. Reprinted as "Norman Mailer's
An American Dream" in Beyond All This Fiddle:
Essays 1955-67. New York: Random House,
1969, pp. 213-17.

Bannon, B. A. "Fiction." Publishers' Weekly, 180
(January 24, 1966), 314.

Barrett, William. "Reader's Choice." Atlantic,
April, 1965, pp. 152-54.

Bersani, Leo. "The Interpretation of Dreams."
Partisan Review, 32 (Fall, 1965), 603-08. Re-
printed in Norman Mailer: A Collection of
Critical Essays, ed. Leo Braudy. Englewood
Cliffs, New Jersey: Prentice-Hall, 1972,
pp. 120-26; and in Norman Mailer: The Man
and His Work, ed. Robert F. Lucid. Boston:
Little, Brown, 1971, pp. 171-79.

Bienen, L. B. Transition, 5 (1971), 20-26.

Bissett, Bill. Canadian Forum, July, 1967, pp. 92-93.

Booklist, 61 (May 16, 1965), 906.

Boroff, David. " 'American Dream,' A Demonic
Fantasy, Shows Norman Mailer at his Worst."
National Observer, March 15, 1965, p. 20.

_____. "American Dream; Review Essay His
'Ragged Edge' [sic]." American Judaism, 14
(Summer, 1965), 12+.

Cayton, Robert F. "Fiction." Library Journal, 90
(March 15, 1965), 1349-50.

Choice, 2 (July-August, 1965), 299.

Coleman, John. Observer, April, 1965, p. 27.

Coleman, Terry. "American Dreamer." Guardian, April 26, 1965, p. 7.

Coren, Alan. "Portrait of the Artist as a Young Executive." Atlas, August, 1965, pp. 110-12.

Corke, Hilary. "New Fiction." The Listener, 73 (April 29, 1965), 645.

Corrington, John William. "An American Dreamer." Chicago Review, 18 (1965), 58-66.

Dana, Robert. "The Harbors of the Moon." North American Review, 2 (July, 1965), 56-57.

Didion, Joan. "A Social Eye." National Review, 17 (April 20, 1965), 329-30.

Dolbier, M. New York Herald Tribune, March 15, 1965, p. 25.

Edinborough, A. Saturday Night, May, 1965, p. 29.

Epstein, Joseph. "Norman X: The Literary Man's Cassius Clay." New Republic, April 17, 1965, pp. 22-25.

Foot, M. Books and Bookmen, November 12, 1966, p. 66.

Fremont-Smith, Eliot. New York Times, March 17, 1965, p. 47.

Fuller, Edmund. Wall Street Journal, April 23, 1965, p. 8.

Green, Howard. "Reviews." Hudson Review, 18 (Summer, 1965), 286-89.

Hardwick, Elizabeth. "Bad Boy." Partisan Review,
    32 (Spring, 1965), 291-94. Reprinted as "A
    Nightmare by Norman Mailer" in Norman Mailer:
    The Man and His Work, ed. Robert F. Lucid.
    Boston: Little, Brown, 1971, pp. 145-50.

Hicks, Granville. "A Literary Hoax?" Saturday Re-
    view, March 20, 1965, pp. 23-24. Reprinted
    in Literary Horizons: A Quarter Century of
    American Fiction. New York: New York Uni-
    versity Press, 1970, pp. 278-83.

_____. "A Matter of Critical Opinion." Saturday
    Review, August 7, 1965, p. 19.

Hux, Samuel. "Mailer's Dream of Violence." Minne-
    sota Review, 8 (1968), 152-97.

Hyman, Stanley Edgar. "Norman Mailer's Yummy
    Rump." New Leader, March 15, 1965, pp. 16-
    17. Reprinted in Standards: A Chronicle of
    Books for Our Time. New York: Horizon Press,
    1966, pp. 275-78; and in Norman Mailer: A
    Collection of Critical Essays, ed. Leo Braudy.
    Englewood Cliffs, New Jersey: Prentice-Hall,
    1972, pp. 104-08.

"In Carcinoma City." Times Literary Supplement,
    3296 (April 29, 1965), 325.

Kazin, Alfred. "Imagination and the Age." Reporter,
    May 5, 1966, pp. 32-35.

Kermode, Frank. "Rammel." New Statesman, 69
    (May 14, 1965), 765-66.

Kirkus, 33 (February 1, 1965), 123.

Knickerbocker, Conrad. "A Man Desperate for a New
    Life." New York Times Book Review, March 14,
    1965, pp. 1, 36, 38-39.

McAllen, J. J. Best Seller, 24 (March 15, 1965), 481.

Maddocks, Melvin. Christian Science Monitor, April 1,
    1965, p. 11.

Matz, Charles. "Mailer's Opera." Opera News,
    February 21, 1970, pp. 14-16.

Maxwell, Robert. "Personal Reactions to a Presiden-
    tial Candidate." Minnesota Review, 5 (August-
    October, 1965), 244-54.

Muste, John M. "Nightmarish Mailer." Progressive,
    February, 1965, pp. 49-51.

Newsweek, December 27, 1965, p. 72.

Nolte, W. H. Northwest Review, 7 (Spring-Summer,
    1965), 76-80.

"Noxious Nostrum." Newsweek, March 15, 1965,
    pp. 101-02.

Observer, August 28, 1966, p. 14.

Petersen, Clarence. Books Today, March 27, 1966,
    p. 10.

Pickerel, Paul. "Thing of Darkness." Harper's,
    April, 1965, pp. 116-17.

Poirier, Richard. "Morbid-mindedness." Commentary,
    June, 1965, pp. 91-94. Reprinted in Norman
    Mailer: The Man and His Work, ed. Robert F.
    Lucid. Boston: Little, Brown, 1971, pp. 162-
    70.

Pollock, V. Punch, 248 (May 19, 1965), 752.

"The Public Act." Time, March 19, 1965, p. 112.

Raab, Lawrence. American Scholar, 37 (Summer,
    1968), 540.

Rahv, Philip. "Crime Without Punishment." New

York Review of Books, March 25, 1965, pp. 1,
3, 4. Reprinted in The Myth and the Power-
house. New York: Farrar, Straus and Giroux,
1965, pp. 234-43, and in Literature and the
Sixth Sense. Boston: Houghton Mifflin, 1970,
pp. 409-17.

Richler, Mordecai. "Norman Mailer." Encounter,
July, 1965, pp. 61-64.

Ricks, Christopher. "Saint Stephen." New Statesman,
69 (April 30, 1965), 687.

Sadoya, Shigenobu. Studies of American Novels: Norman Mailer Number (Japan), 1 (May 25, 1973).

Schlueter, Paul. "American Nightmare." Christian
Century, 132 (May, 1965), 659-60.

Smith, W. G. Books and Bookmen, May, 1965, p. 6.

Spender, Stephen. "Mailer's American Melodrama" in
The Great Ideas Today, 1965, ed. Robert M.
Hutchins and Mortimer J. Adler. Chicago: En-
cyclopaedia Brittanica, 1965, pp. 166-77.

Tanner, Tony. "The Great American Nightmare."
Spectator, 7192 (April 29, 1966), 530-31.

Virginia Quarterly Review, 41 (Summer, 1965), lxxxii.

Wagenheim, Allan J. "Square's Progress: An American Dream." Critique, 10 (Winter, 1968), 45-68.

Weber, Brom. "A Fear of Dying: Norman Mailer's
An American Dream." Hollins Critic, June,
1965, pp. 1-6, 8-11.

Wolfe, Tom. "Son of Crime and Punishment; Or,
How to Go Eight Fast Rounds with the Heavy-
weight Champ--and Lose." Book Week, March 14,
1965, pp. 1, 10, 12-13. Reprinted in Norman
Mailer: The Man and His Work, ed. Robert F.

Lucid. Boston: Little, Brown, 1971, pp. 151-
61.

Cannibals and Christians (1966)

Aldridge, John W. "Victim and Analyst." Commen-
tary, October, 1966, pp. 131-33. Reprinted as
"Cannibals and Christians" in The Devil in the
Fire: Essays in American Literature and Cul-
ture 1951-1971. New York: Harper's Magazine
Press, 1971, pp. 180-84.

Alvarez, A. "Dr. Mailer, I Presume." Observer,
October 15, 1967, p. 27.

Bergonzi, B. London Magazine, November, 1968,
p. 98.

Cayton, Robert F. "Literature." Library Journal,
91 (August, 1966), 3730.

Darack, Arthur. "Man Against His Times." Saturday
Review, September 3, 1966, p. 35.

Donoghue, Denis. "O Mailer, O America." The
Listener, 78 (October 19, 1967), 505-06.

"Feeling the Truth." Time, September 2, 1966,
pp. 82-83.

Fremont-Smith, Eliot. "A Nobel for Norman?" New
York Times, August 22, 1966, p. 31.

Fuller, Edmund. Wall Street Journal, August 31,
1966, p. 10.

Giles, William E. "Mailer's Manner: Charm in a
Raging Style." National Observer, September 19,
1966, p. 25.

Gilmore, T. B. "Fury of a Hebrew Prophet." North
American Review, 251 (November, 1966), 43-44.

Green, Martin. "The Way of the Cannibal." Manchester Guardian, October 26, 1967, p. 10.

Handlin, Oscar. "The Artist and Society." Atlantic,
October, 1966, p. 144.

Kirkus, 34 (July 15, 1966), 720.

Kitching, Jessie. "Nonfiction." Publishers' Weekly,
July 25, 1966, p. 68.

Krim, Seymour. "An Open Letter to Norman Mailer."
Evergreen Review, February, 1967, pp. 89-96.
Reprinted in Shake It for the World Smartass.
New York: Dell, 1970, pp. 111-19.

Lindroth, James R. "Book Reviews." America, 115
(October, 1966), 393.

Maddocks, Melvin. Christian Science Monitor,
August 25, 1966, p. 7.

May, D. The Listener (April 3, 1969), 467.

Muggeridge, Malcolm. "Books." Esquire, December,
1966, pp. 104, 106.

Newsweek, December 19, 1966, p. 118.

Novak, Michael. Critic, 25 (December, 1966-
January, 1967), 81.

"Pasta Fazool." Newsweek, August 29, 1966, p. 73.

Petersen, Clarence. "We Wuz Robbed." Book World,
November 5, 1967, p. 21.

Price, R. G. Punch, January 3, 1968, p. 31.

Pritchard, William H. "Norman Mailer's Extrava-
gances." Massachusetts Review, 8 (Summer,
1967), 562-68.

Publishers' Weekly, July 31, 1967, p. 58.

Richler, Mordecai. "Ex-champ." Spectator, 219
     (October 27, 1967), 504.

Rosenthal, Raymond. "Mailer's Mafia: The Journalism
     of a Writer Who is in Danger of Becoming His
     Audience." Book Week, September 4, 1966,
     pp. 1, 14.

Samuels, Charles T. "Mailer vs. the Hilton Hotel."
     National Review, 18 (October 18, 1966), 1059-60,
     1062.

Sheed, Wilfred. Books Today, August 21, 1966, p. 3.

_____. "One-man Dance Marathon." New York
     Times Book Review, August 21, 1966, pp. 1, 33.

Tanner, Tony. "In the Lion's Den." Partisan Re-
     view, 34 (Summer, 1967), 465-71.

Thompson, John. "Catching Up on Mailer." New
     York Review of Books, April 20, 1967, pp. 14-
     16.

Times Literary Supplement (September 2, 1966), 82.

Tracy, R. Southern Review (Summer, 1970), 890.

Virginia Quarterly Review, 43 (Spring, 1967), xc.

Wain, John. "Mailer's America." New Republic,
     October 1, 1966, pp. 19-20.

Weinberg, Helen. Midstream (November, 1966), 78.

          The Bullfight: A Photographic Narrative
          with Text by Norman Mailer (1967)

Patterson, William. "Bullfight." Saturday Review,
     January 13, 1967, p. 105.

Pearson, A. Manchester Guardian, February 27, 1968,
     p. 10.

Weisenberg, C. M. Library Journal, 93 (February 1,
     1968), 567.

The Deer Park: A Play (1967) [book]
(for play reviews see "Reviews and
Articles on Plays and Films")

Baker, Robert. "Theater." Library Journal, 92
     (July, 1967), 657-58.

"Fiction." Publishers' Weekly, May 15, 1967, p. 42.

Petersen, Clarence. Books Today, June 25, 1967.

Thompson, John. "Catching Up on Mailer." New York
     Review of Books, April 20, 1967, pp. 14-16.

The Short Fiction of Norman Mailer (1967)

Petersen, Clarence. Books Today, May 14, 1967,
     p. 10.

Publishers' Weekly, March 27, 1967, p. 62.

Why Are We in Vietnam? (1967)

Adams, Phoebe. "Potpourri." Atlantic, October,
     1967, pp. 143-44.

Aldridge, John W. "From Vietnam to Obscenity."
     Harper's, February, 1968, pp. 91-97. Reprinted
     in The Devil in the Fire: Essays on American
     Literature and Culture, 1951-1971. New York:
     Harper's Magazine Press, 1971, pp. 185-94; and
     in Norman Mailer: The Man and His Work, ed.
     Robert F. Lucid. Boston: Little, Brown, 1971,
     pp. 180-92.

Broyard, Anatole. "A Disturbance of the Peace." New York Times Book Review, September 17, 1967, pp. 4-5.

Capitanchik, Maurice. "Over-exposed." Spectator (April 11, 1969), 476.

Christian Science Monitor, September 14, 1967, p. 13.

Cook, Bruce. National Observer, September 18, 1967, p. 23.

Dommergues, Pierre. "Norman Mailer: Pourquoi Sommes-nous au Vietnam?" Langues Modernes, 62 (1968), 123-28.

Donoghue, Denis. "Sweepstakes." New York Review of Books, September 28, 1967, pp. 5-6.

Duffy, Dennis. "Books Reviewed." Canadian Forum, May, 1968, p. 44.

Eimerl, Sarel. "Loaded for Bear." Reporter, October 19, 1967, pp. 42-44.

Epstein, Joseph. "Mailer Rides Again: Brilliant, Idiosyncratic, Unquotable." Book World, September 10, 1967, pp. 1, 34.

"Fiction." Publishers' Weekly, July 31, 1967, p. 52; April 22, 1968, p. 54.

Fremont-Smith, Eliot. "Norman Mailer's Cherry Pie." New York Times, September 8, 1967, p. 41M.

Fuller, Edmund. Wall Street Journal, September 21, 1967, p. 16.

Hassan, Ihab. "Focus on Norman Mailer's Why Are We in Vietnam?" in American Dreams, American Nightmares, ed. David Madden. Carbondale: Southern Illinois University Press, 1970, pp. 197-203.

Hicks, Granville. "Lark in the Race for the Presi-
    dency." Saturday Review, September 16, 1967,
    pp. 39-40. Reprinted in Literary Horizons: A
    Quarter Century of American Fiction. New York:
    New York University Press, 1970, pp. 283-86.

_____. "Five for the Year's End." Saturday Re-
    view, December 30, 1967, pp. 19-20.

Hope, F. New Statesman (April 4, 1969), 476.

"Huntsville Public Library Rocked by Mailer Book."
    Library Journal, 93 (January 15, 1968), 138.

Kauffmann, Stanley. "An American Dreamer." New
    Republic, September 16, 1967, p. 18.

Kaufmann, Donald L. "Catch-23: The Mystery of
    Fact (Norman Mailer's Final Novel?)." Twentieth
    Century Literature, 17 (October, 1971), 247-56.

Kirkus, 35 (July 15, 1967), 830.

Kroll, Jack. "The Scrambler." Newsweek, Septem-
    ber 18, 1967.

Lehan, Richard. "Fiction, 1967." Contemporary
    Literature, 9 (Autumn, 1968), 538-53.

Lehmann-Haupt, Christopher. "Norman Mailer as
    Joycean Punster and Manipulator of Language."
    Commonweal, 87 (December 8, 1967), 338-39.

Lindroth, James R. "Book Reviews." America, 117
    (September 30, 1967), 356.

Maud, Ralph. "Faulkner, Mailer, and Yogi Bear."
    Canadian Review of American Studies, 2 (Fall,
    1971), 69-75.

May, D. The Listener (April 3, 1969), 467.

Moon, Eric. "Fiction." Library Journal, 92

(September 15, 1967), 3056-57.

Morel, Jean-Pierre. "Pourquois sommes-nous au Vietnam?" Études, 329 (1968), 572-80.

Nichols, Christopher. "Psychedelic Freakout." National Review, 19 (October 31, 1967), 1216-17.

Pearce, Richard. "Norman Mailer's Why Are We in Vietnam?: A Radical Critique of Frontier Values." Modern Fiction Studies, 17 (Autumn, 1971), 409-14.

Petersen, Clarence. Book World, June 16, 1968, p. 13.

Publishers' Weekly, April 22, 1968, p. 54.

Ramsey, Roger. "Current and Recurrent: The Vietnam Novel." Modern Fiction Studies, 17 (Autumn, 1971), 415-32.

Rosenthal, Raymond. "America's No. 1 Disc Jockey." New Leader, September 25, 1967, pp. 16-17.

Sale, Roger. "Reviews." Hudson Review, 20 (Winter, 1967-68), 669-70.

Samuels, Charles T. "The Novel, U.S.A.: Mailerrhea." Nation, 205 (October 23, 1967), 405-06.

Schott, Webster. "Mailer Writes Dirty about the Aurora Borealis." Life, September 15, 1967, p. 8.

Time, September 8, 1967, p. D12.

Times Literary Supplement (April 3, 1969), 341.

Toback, James. Time (Chicago), September 8, 1967, sec. D, p. 12.

Tucker, Martin. Commonweal, 87 (December 1, 1967),
    315.

Wallenstein, B. Catholic World, January, 1968, p. 189.

                The Armies of the Night (1968)

Alvarez, A. "Reflections in a Bloodshot Eye." New
    Statesman, 76 (September 20, 1968), 351-52.

Berthoff, Warner. "Witness and Testament: Two
    Contemporary Classics" in Fictions and Events.
    New York: Dutton, 1971, pp. 288-308. Re-
    printed in Aspects of Narrative, ed. J. Hillis
    Miller. New York: Columbia University Press,
    1971, pp. 173-98.

Boston, Richard. "Heroes and Villains." New Society,
    12 (September 19, 1968), 419-20.

Braudy, Leo. "Advertisements for a Dwarf Alter-ego."
    New Journal, 1 (May 12, 1968), 7-9.

Brown, Charles H. "Journalism Versus Art." Cur-
    rent, June, 1972, pp. 31-38.

Canadian Forum, July, 1968, p. 84.

Champoli, John D. "Norman Mailer and The Armies
    of the Night." Massachusetts Studies in English,
    3 (1971), 17-21.

Commonweal (June 7, 1968), 362.

Davis, Douglas M. "Mr. Mailer as Comic Hero of
    Pentagon March." National Observer, May 6,
    1968, p. 21.

De'Ath, W. Punch, 255 (October 2, 1968), 482.

"First Person Singular." Time, February 23, 1968,
    p. 81.

Frank, Armin P.   "Literarische Strukturbegriffe und
    Norman Mailers The Armies of the Night."
    Jahrbuch für Amerikastudien, 17:   73-99.

Fremont-Smith, Eliot.   "Mailer on the March."   New
    York Times, April 26, 1968, p. 41.

Gilman, Richard.   "What Mailer Has Done."   New
    Republic, June 8, 1968, pp. 27-31.   Reprinted
    in Representative Men, ed. Theodore L. Gross.
    New York: Free Press, 1970, pp. 217-26;   and
    in Norman Mailer: A Collection of Critical
    Essays, ed. Leo Braudy.   Englewood Cliffs,
    New Jersey: Prentice-Hall, 1972, pp. 158-66.

Greenfield, Josh.   "Line Between Journalism and
    Literature Thin, Perhaps, But Distinct."   Com-
    monweal, 88 (June 7, 1968), 362-63.

Hart, Jeffrey.   "Anti-Matter as Jet Set Journalism."
    National Review, 20 (July 30, 1968), 754-55.

Hicks, Granville.   Saturday Review, December 28,
    1968.   Reprinted in Literary Horizons: A Quar-
    ter Century of American Fiction.   New York:
    New York University Press, 1970, pp. 287-90.

Janeway, William.   "Mailer's America."   Cambridge
    Review, November 29, 1968, pp. 183-85.

Jones, D. A. N.   "Embattled Image."   The Listener,
    80 (September 26, 1968), 405-06.

Kazin, Alfred.   "The Trouble He's Seen."   New York
    Times Book Review, May 5, 1968, pp. 1-2, 26.

Kirkus, 36 (March 15, 1968), 373;   (April 1, 1968),
    411.

Lipton, Lawrence.   "Norman Mailer: genius, novelist,
    critic, playwright, politico, journalist, and gen-
    eral all-around shit."   Los Angeles Free Press,
    May 31, 1968, pp. 27-28.

Macdonald, Dwight. "Politics." Esquire, May, 1968,
     pp. 41, 42, 44, 194, 196; June, 1968, pp. 46,
     48, 50, 183.

MacIntyre, A. Guardian, September 26, 1968, p. 31.

McKenzie, J. L. Critic, August-September, 1968,
     p. 8.

Maddocks, Melvin. "Norm's Ego is Working Overtime
     for YOU." Life, May 10, 1968, p. 8.

Maloff, Saul. "The Tenth Man." Newsweek, May 6,
     1968, pp. 107-08.

Merideth, Robert. "The 45-second Piss: A Left
     Critique of Norman Mailer and The Armies of
     the Night." Modern Fiction Studies, 17 (Autumn,
     1971), 433-49.

Middlebrook, Jonathan. "Can a Middle-aged Man with
     Four Wives and Six Children Be a Revolutionary?"
     Journal of Popular Culture, 3 (Winter, 1970),
     565-74.

Moon, Eric. "The Contemporary Scene." Library
     Journal, 93 (June 1, 1968), 2227.

Morris, Willie. "Norman Mailer's The Armies of the
     Night." Literary Guild Magazine, July, 1968,
     p. 15.

Muggeridge, Malcolm. Esquire, July, 1968, pp. 20,
     22.

Newlove, Donald. "Dinner at the Lowells." Esquire,
     September, 1969, pp. 128-29, 168, 170, 176-78,
     180, 184.

Nordell, Roderick. "The Face in Mailer's Mirror."
     Christian Science Monitor, May 16, 1968, p. 11;
     May 20, 1968, p. 5.

"Norman Mailer's March." Times Literary Supplement, September 19, 1968, p. 1050.

"Novelist as Novelist." Economist, November 9, 1968, p. viii.

O'Brien, Conor Cruise. "Confessions of the Last American." New York Review of Books, June 20, 1968, pp. 16-18.

Publishers' Weekly, March 11, 1968, p. 46.

Publishers' Weekly, November 4, 1968, p. 52.

Puzo, Mario. "Generalissimo Mailer: Hero of His Own Dispatches." Book World, April 28, 1968, p. 1.

Raab, L. American Scholar, 37 (Summer, 1968), 540.

Resnik, Harry S. "Hand on the Pulse of America." Saturday Review, May 4, 1968, pp. 25-26.

Sadoya, Shigenobu. Studies of American Novels: Norman Mailer Number (Japan), 1 (May 25, 1973).

Simon, John. "Mailer on the March." Hudson Review, 21 (Autumn, 1968), 541-45.

Smith, Julian. "Toe Deep in Protest." Christian Century, 85 (August 14, 1968), 1020.

"Surveying Supernation." Newsweek, February 26, 1968, p. 62.

"Ten of Particular Significance and Excellence in 1968." New York Times Book Review, December 1, 1968, p. 1.

Thompson, R. J. America, July 6, 1968, p. 18.

Toynbee, P. Observer, September 22, 1968, p. 31.

"The Weekend Revolution." Time, May 10, 1968,
    pp. 120-124.

The Idol and the Octopus (1968)

Petersen, Clarence. Book World, July 21, 1968,
    p. 13.

Publishers' Weekly, May 27, 1968, p. 59.

Miami and the Siege of Chicago (1968)

Buckley, Priscilla. National Review, 21 (February 11,
    1969), 129.

Economist, November 23, 1968, p. 71.

Fremont-Smith, Eliot. "Family Report." New York
    Times, October 28, 1968, p. 45.

Fuller, Edmund. Wall Street Journal, December 20,
    1968, p. 14.

Halberstam, Michael. "Norman Mailer as Ethnog-
    rapher." Trans-Action, March, 1969, pp. 71-72.

"Mailer's America." Time, October 1, 1968, pp. 81-
    82.

Mitchell, Julian. New Statesman, 76 (November 22,
    1968), 716.

Nyren, Karl. Library Journal, 94 (January 1, 1969),
    58.

Publishers' Weekly, October 13, 1968, p. 67.

Richardson, Jack. "The Aesthetics of Norman Mailer."
    New York Review of Books, May 8, 1969, pp. 3-
    4. Reprinted in Norman Mailer: The Man and
    His Work, ed. Robert F. Lucid. Boston: Little,

Brown, 1971, pp. 193-200.

Samuels, Charles T. Book World, November 3, 1968, p. 3.

Shaw, Peter. "The Conventions, 1968." Commentary, December, 1968, pp. 93-96.

Sheed, Wilfred. "Miami and the Siege of Chicago: A Review." New York Times Book Review, December 6, 1968, pp. 3, 56.

Times Literary Supplement (December 5, 1968), 1355.

Trachtenberg, Alan. "Repeat Performance." Nation, 207 (December 9, 1968), 631-32.

Of a Fire on the Moon (1970)

Adams, Phoebe. Atlantic, February, 1971, p. 129.

Bell, Pearl K. "The Power and the Vainglory." New Leader, February 8, 1971, pp. 16-17.

Brudnoy, David. National Review, 23 (January 12, 1971), 38.

Choice, 8 (June, 1971), 537.

DeMott, Benjamin. "Inside Apollo II with Aquarius Mailer." Saturday Review, January 16, 1971, pp. 25-27, 57-58.

Dickstein, Morris. "A Trip to Inner and Outer Space." New York Times Book Review, January 10, 1971, pp. 1, 42-43, 45.

"Downfall of the Prince of Ego." Sunday Times (London), March 14, 1971, pp. 25-26.

Economist, November 28, 1970, p. 52.

Flying, March, 1972, p. 84.

Grigson, Geoffrey. New Statesman, 80 (November 27, 1970), 720.

Kaufmann, Donald. "Mailer's Lunar Bits and Pieces." Modern Fiction Studies, 17 (Autumn, 1971), 451-54.

Kazin, Alfred. "Capote's Kansas and Mailer's Moon." New York Review of Books, April 8, 1971, pp. 26-30.

Kramer, Hilton. Book World, January 10, 1971, p. 1.

Lehmann-Haupt, Christopher. "Mailer's Dream of the Moon--I." New York Times, January 7, 1971, p. 33; "Mailer [sic] Dream of the Moon--II." New York Times, January 8, 1971, p. 29.

Maurer, Harry. Nation, 212 (March 22, 1971), 378.

Moon, Eric. Library Journal, 95 (November 15, 1970), 3918.

"The Moonshot." Observer, August 31, 1969, pp. 17-18.

"The Moonshot. 2. Ship of Flames." Observer, September 7, 1969, p. 25.

Moore, P. The Listener (November 26, 1970), 749.

Murphy, J. M. Best Sellers, 30 (January 15, 1971), 445.

New Yorker, March 13, 1971, p. 136.

Parker, D. L. Christian Science Monitor, January 14, 1971, p. 7.

Poirier, Richard. "Ups and Downs of Mailer." New Republic, January 23, 1971, pp. 23-26. Reprinted in <u>Norman Mailer: A Collection of Critical Essays</u>, ed. Leo Braudy. Englewood Cliffs, New Jersey: Prentice-Hall, 1972, pp. 167-74.

<u>Publishers' Weekly</u>, January 25, 1971, pp. 177-79.

Rowley, Peter. <u>Christian Century</u>, January 20, 1971, p. 76.

Sale, Roger. "Watchman, What of the Night?" <u>New York Review of Books</u>, May 6, 1971, pp. 13-17.

Sargent, Pamela. "The Promise of Space: Transformations of a Dream." <u>Riverside Quarterly</u> (University of Saskatchewan), 5 (1971), 83-88.

Schroth, Raymond A. "Mailer on the Moon." <u>Commonweal</u>, 94 (May 7, 1971), 216-18.

Sheppard, R. Z. <u>Time</u>, January 11, 1971, p. 70.

Sisk, John P. "Aquarius Rising." <u>Commentary</u>, May, 1971, pp. 83-84.

<u>Times Literary Supplement</u> (December 4, 1970), 1425.

Toynbee, Philip. <u>Critic</u>, May, 1971, p. 78.

Werge, Thomas. "An Apocalyptic Voyage: God, Satan, and the American Tradition in Norman Mailer's <u>Of a Fire on the Moon</u>." <u>Review of Politics</u>, October, 1972, pp. 108-28. Reprinted in <u>America in Change</u>, ed. R. E. Weber. South Bend: University of Notre Dame Press, 1972, pp. 108-28.

Wolff, Geoffrey. <u>Newsweek</u>, January 4, 1971, p. 64.

"<u>King of the Hill</u>" (1971)

No citations.

The Prisoner of Sex (1971)

Barnes, Annette. "Norman Mailer: A Prisoner of
    Sex." Massachusetts Review, 13 (Winter, 1972),
    269-74.

Beer, P. The Listener (August 26, 1971), 275.

Berry, John. Library Journal, 96 (June 1, 1971),
    1958.

Books and Bookmen, February, 1972, p. 26.

Brophy, Brigid. "The Prisoner of Sex." New York
    Times Book Review, May 23, 1971, pp. 1, 14,
    16.

_____. "What Katy Did to Norman." Sunday
    Times Magazine (London), September 12, 1971,
    p. 53.

Broyard, Anatole. New York Times, May 27, 1971,
    p. 41.

Carrascal, José Maria. "Norman Mailer, prisionero
    de su mismo." Estafeta Literaria, 478
    (October 15, 1971), 36.

DeMott, Benjamin. Saturday Review, July 10, 1971,
    p. 21.

Economist, August 28, 1971, p. 45.

Greenway, J. "Norman Mailer Meets the Butch
    Brigade." National Review (July 27, 1971), 815.

Hill, W. B. Best Sellers, June 15, 1971, p. 144.

Kennedy, Eugene. Critic, November, 1971, p. 69.

Lodge, David. "Male, Mailer, Female." New Black
    Friars, 52 (December, 1971), 558-61.

Mitchell, Juliet. "Mailer: 'So the revolution called
     again....'" Modern Occasions, 1 (Fall, 1971),
     611-18.

Oates, Joyce Carol. "Out of the Machine." Atlantic,
     July, 1971, pp. 42-45. Reprinted in Will the
     Real Norman Mailer Please Stand Up?, ed.
     Laura Adams. Port Washington, New York:
     Kennikat Press, 1974, pp. 216-23.

"The Poisoner of Sex/N*rm*n Ma*ler." Harvard
     Lampoon Parody of Cosmopolitan, December,
     1972, pp. 62-64, 88-91, 96.

Pritchett, V. S. "With Norman Mailer at the Sex
     Circus: Into the Cage." Atlantic, July, 1971,
     pp. 40-42.

Raban, Jonathan. "Huck Mailer and the Widow Millett."
     New Statesman, 82 (September 3, 1971), 303-04.

Times Literary Supplement (September 17, 1971), 1114.

Wills, Garry. Book World, July 11, 1971, p. 1.

"Women's Lib: Mailer vs. Millett." Time, Feb-
     ruary 22, 1971, p. 71.

Maidstone: A Mystery (1971)

Braudy, Leo. "Maidstone: A Mystery." New York
     Times Book Review, December 19, 1971,
     pp. 2-3, 25. Reprinted in Will the Real Norman
     Mailer Please Stand Up?, ed. Laura Adams.
     Port Washington, New York: Kennikat Press,
     1974, pp. 168-72.

Existential Errands (1972)

Booklist, 68 (July 15, 1972), 966.

Buchanan, Cynthia. New York Times Book Review,
    April 16, 1972, pp. 27-28.

Choice, 9 (October, 1972), 971.

Edwards, Thomas. "Keeping Up with Norman Mailer."
    New York Review of Books, June 15, 1972,
    pp. 21-22.

Haney, R. W. Christian Science Monitor, July 26,
    1972, p. 9.

Heckel, James. Library Journal, 97 (March 15, 1972),
    1016.

Kirkus, 40 (February 15, 1972), 242.

Lask, T. New York Times, May 5, 1972, p. 42.

Maloff, Saul. Commonweal, 96 (June 30, 1972), 361.

New Yorker, June 17, 1972, p. 103.

Oberbeck, S. K. Book World, April 30, 1972, p. 5.

Publishers' Weekly, February 19, 1973, p. 82;
    March 13, 1972, p. 59.

Saturday Review, December 2, 1972, p. 78.

St. George and the Godfather (1972)

Adams, Laura. Leisure Magazine (Dayton Daily News),
    November 19, 1972, p. 10.

America, 127 (November 18, 1972), 425.

Commonweal (December 8, 1972), 232-34.

Cook, Bruce. "Aquarius Rex." National Observer,
    November 4, 1972, pp. 1, 15. Reprinted in
    Will the Real Norman Mailer Please Stand Up?,

ed. Laura Adams. Port Washington, New York: Kennikat Press, 1974. [See also "General Articles and Critiques"].

Hogan, William. Saturday Review, October 21, 1972, p. 80.

Lehmann-Haupt, Christopher. New York Times, October 16, 1972, p. 39.

New Yorker, October 28, 1972, p. 158.

[Review of St. George and the Godfather and Norman Mailer by Richard Poirier.] New York Times, October 16, 1972, p. 35.

Solotaroff, Robert. "The Glop of the Wad." Nation, January 15, 1973, pp. 87-89.

Thorburn, David. "The Artist as Performer." Commentary, April, 1973, pp. 86-88, 90-93.

Time, October 30, 1972, p. 110.

Wills, Garry. "Aquarius Returns to Miami." New York Times Book Review, October 15, 1972, pp. 1, 22.

Marilyn: A Novel Biography (1973)

[Advertisement for Marilyn.] New York Times Book Review, December 9, 1973, pp. 13-15.

Avant, J. A. Library Journal, 98 (August, 1973), 2330.

Berg, Louis. "When She Was Good ... [Review of Marilyn and Marilyn: An Untold Story by Norman Rosten]." Saturday Review/World, September 25, 1973, pp. 32-34.

Book World, August 12, 1973, p. 1.

Clark, Marsh and Stefan Kanfer. "Two Myths Con-
      verge: NM Discovers MM." Time, July 16,
      1973, pp. 60-64, 69-70.

Clemons, Walter. "Double Monroe." Newsweek,
      July 30, 1973, p. 71.

Commentary, (October 1973), 414.

Frelicher, Lila. "Mailer Celebrates Monroe for
      Grosset and Dunlap." Publishers' Weekly,
      November 13, 1972, p. 36.

French, Philip. "Norman and Norma Jean." New
      Statesman (November 9, 1973), 688-89.

Fuller, Edmund. "Mailer's Sexploitation of Marilyn
      [Review of Marilyn and Marilyn: An Untold
      Story by Norman Rosten]." Wall Street Journal,
      September 24, 1973, p. 14.

Hills, R. "Fiction." Esquire, November, 1973,
      pp. 20+.

Kael, Pauline. [Review of Marilyn.] New York
      Times Book Review, July 22, 1973, pp. 1-3.

Kirkus (July 1, 1973), 736.

Lucid, Robert F. "Marilyn by Mailer." Books
      (Philadelphia Bulletin), July 22, 1973, p. 7.

Maloff, Saul. "Mailer's Marilyn." Commonweal, 98
      (September 21, 1973), 503-05.

"Much Ado About Mailer's Marilyn." Publishers'
      Weekly, July 30, 1973, p. 45.

Nation, 217 (October 15, 1973), 376.

New Leader, September 17, 1973, p. 21.

New York Times, July 16, 1973, p. 27; July 17,

1973, p. 37.

New York Times Book Review, August 12, 1973,
    p. 25.

New Yorker, August 6, 1973, p. 87.

Publishers' Weekly, June 25, 1973, p. 70.

Ryan, F. L. Best Sellers, August 15, 1973, p. 222.

Seelye, John. New Republic, September 1, 1973,
    p. 25.

Stafford, J. "Mailer's Marilyn Monroe." Vogue,
    September, 1973, pp. 288-89+.

Sweeney, Louise. Christian Science Monitor,
    August 1, 1973, p. 8.

Weales, Gerald. "The Naked and the Dead." Hudson
    Review, 26 (Winter, 1973-74), 769-72.

Wood, Michael. "Kissing Hitler [Review of Norman
    Mailer by Richard Poirier and Marilyn]." New
    York Review of Books, September 20, 1973,
    pp. 22-24.

The Faith of Graffiti (1974)

Broyard, Anatole. "The Handwriting on the Wall."
    New York Times, May 1, 1974, p. 49.

Fremont-Smith, Eliot. "Mailer on the IRT." New
    York, May 6, 1974, pp. 97-98.

"Mailer's Text-with-Pictures: Praeger's Graffiti."
    Publishers' Weekly, February 11, 1974, p. 44.

Robins, Corinne. [Review of] The Faith of Graffiti.
    New York Times Book Review, May 5, 1974,
    p. 51.

B. REVIEWS AND ARTICLES
ON PLAYS AND FILMS

1. PLAYS

The Deer Park

Clurman, Harold. "Theatre." Nation (February 20, 1967), 252-53.

Gilman, Richard. "Big Red Heart." Newsweek, February 13, 1967, pp. 109-09A.

Hewes, Henry. "Hell is Murky." Saturday Review, March 4, 1967, p. 45.

Kerr, Walter. "Norman Mailer's Wicked 'Deer Park'." New York Times, February 1, 1967, p. 27.

"The Naked and the Damned." Time, February 10, 1967, p. 58.

Oliver, Edith. "The Theatre." New Yorker, February 11, 1967, p. 116.

Sheed, Wilfred. "Another Word from the Sponsor." Life, February 24, 1967, p. 8.

Smith, William James. "A Novel Play." Commonweal, 85 (March 10, 1967), 657-58.

Vogue, April 1, 1967, p. 94.

Weales, Gerald. "The Park in the Playhouse."

Reporter, April 6, 1967, 47-48. Reprinted in
Will the Real Norman Mailer Please Stand Up?,
ed. Laura Adams. Port Washington, New York:
Kennikat Press, 1974, pp. 163-167.

_____. The Jumping-off Place: American Drama
in the 1960's. New York: Macmillan, 1969,
pp. 218-21.

DJ

No Citations.

2. FILMS

Wild 90

Kael, Pauline. "The Current Cinema: Celebrities
Make Spectacles of Themselves." New Yorker,
January 20, 1968, pp. 90, 92-95.

Kauffmann, Stanley. "Wild 90" in Figures of Light:
Film Criticism and Comment. New York:
Harper & Row, 1971, pp. 49-50.

New York Times, January 8, 1968, p. 33.

Beyond the Law

Byro. Variety, October 2, 1968.

Canby, Vincent. "Norman Mailer Offers Beyond the
Law." New York Times, September 30, 1968.

Hatch, Robert. "Films." Nation, 207 (November 11,
1968), 508.

Kauffmann, Stanley. New Republic, November 16,
1968, p. 18. Reprinted in Figures of Light.
New York: Harper & Row, 1971, pp. 115-17.

Sarris, Andrew. Confessions of a Cultist: On the
     Cinema, 1955-1969. New York: Simon &
     Schuster, 1970, pp. 396-400.

                         Maidstone

Beauman, Sally. "Norman Mailer, Filmmaker." New
     York, 1968.

Cain, Scott. " 'Maidstone' Wild and Funny." Atlanta
     Journal, February 11, 1972, p. 21-A.

Canby, Vincent. "Film: Mailer's 'Maidstone' Opens
     Whitney Series." New York Times, September 24,
     1971, p. 31.

_____. "Norman Mailer--An Ego to Cherish." New
     York Times, September 26, 1971, pp. 1, 5
     [Drama section].

Lee, John M. "Mailer, in London, Trades Jabs with
     Audience Over New Film." New York Times,
     October 17, 1970, p. 21.

Lukas, J. Anthony. "Norman Mailer Enlists His Pri-
     vate Army to Act in Film." New York Times,
     July 23, 1968, p. 41.

_____. "Mailer Film Party a Real Bash: 1 Broken
     Jaw, 2 Bloody Heads." New York Times,
     July 31, 1968, p. 29.

"Mailer Opening." New Yorker, October 2, 1971, p. 33.

"Norman's Phantasmagoria." Time, November 14,
     1971, pp. 97-98.

Roddy, Joseph. "The Latest Model Mailer." Look,
     May 27, 1969, pp. 22-28.

Schickel, R. "Stars and Celebrities." Commentary,
     August, 1971, pp. 61-65.

Toback, James. "At Play in the Fields of the Bored."
    Esquire, December, 1968, pp. 150-55, 22, 24,
    26, 28, 30, 32, 34, 36.

C.   REVIEWS OF WORKS ABOUT MAILER

Aldridge, John W.   "The Perfect Absurd Figure of a
Mighty Absurd Crusade" [Review of Norman
Mailer: The Man and His Work and The Long
Patrol, ed. Robert F. Lucid]. Saturday Review,
November 13, 1971, pp. 45-46, 48-49, 72.

Brooks, Charles W.   "The Fifth Candidate" [Review of
Managing Mailer by Joe Flaherty]. Commentary,
October, 1970, pp. 89-92.

Cooper, Arthur.   "Managing Mailer." Saturday Review, June 6, 1970, p. 36.

Edwards, Thomas.   "Keeping Up with Norman Mailer"
[Review of The Long Patrol and Norman Mailer:
The Man and His Work, ed. Robert F. Lucid
and Existential Errands]. New York Review of
Books, June 15, 1972, pp. 21-22.

Gelfant, Blanche H.   [Review of The Performing Self
by Richard Poirier]. Contemporary Literature,
14 (Spring, 1973), 253-59.

Gilman, Richard.   [Review of Norman Mailer by
Richard Poirier]. New York Times Book Review,
December 17, 1972, pp. 6-7.

Heister, John W.   "Flamboyant Personality" [Review of
The Structured Vision of Norman Mailer by Barry
Leeds and Norman Mailer: The Countdown by
Donald L. Kaufmann]. Christian Century,
January 7, 1970, pp. 20-21.

Hentoff, Margot. "The Boys" [Review of Managing
     Mailer by Joe Flaherty and The Gang Who
     Couldn't Shoot Straight by Jimmy Breslin]. New
     York Review of Books, September 24, 1970,
     p. 17.

Lucid, Robert F. [Review of Norman Mailer: The
     Countdown by Donald Kaufmann, The Structured
     Vision of Norman Mailer by Barry Leeds, Run-
     ning Against the Machine, ed. Peter Manso and
     Managing Mailer by Joe Flaherty]. American
     Literature, 42 (January, 1971), 606-07.

_____. [Review of Norman Mailer by Richard
     Poirier]. Studies in the Novel, 5 (Summer,
     1973), 263.

Pritchett, V. S. [Review of Bright Book of Life:
     American Novelists and Storytellers from
     Hemingway to Mailer by Alfred Kazin]. New
     York Times Book Review, May 20, 1973, p. 3.

Reeves, Richard. "See How They Run: A Review of
     Managing Mailer." New York Times Book Re-
     view, July 19, 1970, pp. 10, 12, 14.

[Review of The Long Patrol, ed. Robert F. Lucid].
     Booklist, 68 (February 1, 1972), 449.

[Review of St. George and the Godfather and Norman
     Mailer by Richard Poirier]. New York Times,
     October 16, 1972, p. 35.

Sale, Roger. "Wrestling with Fiction" [Review of
     Bright Book of Life: American Novelists and
     Storytellers from Hemingway to Mailer by Alfred
     Kazin]. New York Review of Books, March 21,
     1974, pp. 36-37.

Schulz, Max F. "Norman Mailer" [Review of Norman
     Mailer: The Countdown by Donald L. Kaufmann
     and The Structured Vision of Norman Mailer by
     Barry Leeds]. Contemporary Literature, 13
     (Spring, 1972), 243-48.

Tanner, Tony. [Review of The Performing Self by
    Richard Poirier]. New York Times Book Review,
    May 30, 1971, pp. 5, 19.

Thorburn, David. "The Artist as Performer" [Review
    of Norman Mailer by Richard Poirier and St.
    George and the Godfather]. Commentary, April,
    1973, pp. 86-88, 90-93.

Waldmeir, Joseph J. "Running with Mailer" [Review
    of Norman Mailer: The Countdown by Donald
    Kaufmann, The Structured Vision of Norman
    Mailer by Barry Leeds, and Running Against the
    Machine, ed. Peter Manso]. Journal of Modern
    Literature, 1 (March, 1971), 454-57.

Wood, Michael. "Kissing Hitler" [Review of Norman
    Mailer by Richard Poirier and Marilyn]. New
    York Review of Books, September 20, 1973,
    pp. 22-24.

D. GENERAL ARTICLES AND CRITIQUES

Aaron, Jonathan. "Existential Sheriff." The New Journal, 1 (December 10, 1967), 6-7.

Adams, Laura. "Introduction" in Will the Real Norman Mailer Please Stand Up?, ed. Laura Adams. Port Washington, New York: Kennikat Press, 1974, pp. 3-9.

Adelson, Alan M. "Candidate Mailer: Savior or Spoiler?" New Leader, June 9, 1969, pp. 14-16.

Aldridge, John W. In Search of Heresy: American Literature in an Age of Conformity. New York: McGraw-Hill, 1956.

_____. After the Lost Generation. New York: Noonday Press, 1958, pp. 133-41 et passim.

_____. "What Became of Our Postwar Hopes?" New York Times Book Review, July 29, 1962, pp. 1, 24. Reprinted as "The War Writers Ten Years Later" in Contemporary American Novelists, ed. Harry T. Moore. Carbondale: Southern Illinois University Press, 1964.

_____. "Norman Mailer: The Energy of New Success" in Time to Murder and Create: The Contemporary Novel in Crisis. New York: David McKay, 1966, pp. 149-63. Reprinted in Norman Mailer: A Collection of Critical Essays, ed. Leo Braudy. Englewood Cliffs, New Jersey: Prentice-Hall, 1972, pp. 109-19; and in The Devil in the

Fire: Essays in American Literature and Culture
1951-1971. New York: Harper's Magazine Press,
1971, pp. 169-79.

Allen, Walter. The Urgent West: The American
Dream and Modern Man. New York: E. P.
Dutton, 1969.

Alter, Robert. "The Real and Imaginary Worlds of
Norman Mailer." Midstream, January, 1969,
pp. 24-35. Reprinted as "Norman Mailer" in
The Politics of Twentieth-century Novelists, ed.
G. A. Panichas. New York: Hawthorne, 1971,
pp. 321-24.

Alvarez, A. The New Review, 1 (April, 1974).

"American Literature Today: Interview with M. L.
Rosenthal, Part 1." Nation (April 17, 1972),
503-06.

"Americana: Of Time and the Rebel." Time, December 5, 1960, pp. 16-17.

Arlen, Michael J. "Notes on the New Journalism."
Atlantic, May, 1972, pp. 43-77.

Arnavon, Cyrille. "Les Cauchemars de Norman
Mailer." Europe, 47 (January, 1969), 93-116.

Auchincloss, Louis. "The Novel as a Forum." New
York Times Book Review, October 24, 1965, p. 2.

Bakker, J. "Literature, Politics, and Norman Mailer."
Dutch Quarterly Review of Anglo-American Letters,
3-4 (1971), 129-45.

Barksdale, Richard K. "Alienation and the Anti-hero
in Recent American Fiction." College Language
Association Journal, 10 (1966), 1-10.

Baumbach, Jonathan, ed. The Landscape of Nightmare:
Studies in the Contemporary American Novel.

New York: New York University Press, 1965, pp. 1-15.

Beaver, Harold. "A Figure in the Carpet: Irony and the American Novel." English Association Essays and Studies, 15 (1962), 101-14.

Bell, Pearl K. "American Fiction: Forgetting the Ordinary Truths." Dissent (Winter, 1973), 26-34 passim.

Bellow, Saul. "Culture Now." Intellectual Digest, September, 1971, pp. 74-80.

Berman, Ronald. America in the Sixties: An Intellectual History. New York: Free Press, 1968.

Bersani, Leo. "The Agony of the Novel." New Republic, June 8, 1968, pp. 32-34.

Blotner, Joseph. The Modern American Political Novel, 1900-1960. Austin: University of Texas Press, 1966, pp. 320-22 et passim.

Bondy, François. "Norman Mailer oder Inside von Gut und Böse." Merkur, 25 (May, 1971), 449-60.

Bosworth, Patricia. "Fifth Estate at the Four Seasons." Saturday Review of the Arts, March, 1973, pp. 5-7.

Bradner, Tim. "Mailer on Alaska." Alaska Living, Anchorage Daily News, June 30, 1968, pp. 3, 5, 23.

Braudy, Leo. "Baldwin and the White Man's Guilt." The Phoenix, March 3, 1963, pp. 1-3.

_____. "Norman Mailer: The Pride of Vulnerability" in Norman Mailer: A Collection of Critical Essays, ed. Leo Braudy. Englewood Cliffs, New Jersey: Prentice-Hall, 1972, pp. 1-20.

_____, ed. Norman Mailer: A Collection of Critical
    Essays (Twentieth Century Interpretations). Engle-
    wood Cliffs, New Jersey: Prentice-Hall, 1972.

Brezianu, Andrei. "Focul şi gîndul." Secolul XX, 15
    (iii-iv), 266-73.

Bromwich, David. "Some American Masks." Dissent
    (Winter, 1973), 37-39, 44.

Brookman, C. E. "Norman Mailer." Times Literary
    Supplement (October 3, 1968), 1104.

Brooks, Peter. "The Melodramatic Imagination."
    Partisan Review (1972).

Brower, Brock. "Always the Challenger." Life,
    September 24, 1965, pp. 94-96, 98, 100, 102-15,
    117.

Brower, Reuben A. , ed. Twentieth Century Literature
    in Retrospect, Vol. II. Cambridge: Harvard
    University Press, 1973.

Brown, C. H. "Rise of the New Journalism." Cur-
    rent, June, 1972, pp. 31-38.

Brustein, Robert. "Who's Killing the Novel?" New
    Republic, October 23, 1965, pp. 22-24.

_____. "If an Artist Wants to be Serious and Re-
    spected and Rich, Famous and Popular, He is Suf-
    fering from Cultural Schizophrenia." New York
    Times Magazine, September 26, 1971, pp. 12-13,
    85-89.

Bryant, Jerry H. "The Last of the Social Protest
    Writers." Arizona Quarterly, 19 (Winter, 1963),
    315-25.

_____. The Open Decision: The Contemporary
    American Novel and Its Intellectual Background.
    New York: Free Press, 1970, pp. 369-94 et
    passim.

Burdick, Eugene. "Innocent Nihilists Adrift in Squares-ville." Reporter, April 3, 1958, pp. 30-33.

Burgess, Anthony. "The Post-war American Novel: A View from the Periphery." American Scholar, 35 (Winter, 1965-66), 150-58.

_____. "War's Sour Fruits" in The Novel Now: A Student's Guide to Contemporary Fiction. London: Faber and Faber, 1967, pp. 48-51.

Cimatti, P. "L'inferno di Mailer." Fiera Letteraria, April 12, 1959, p. 4.

Cleaver, Eldrige. "Notes on a Native Son." Ramparts, June, 1966, pp. 51-52, 54-56. Reprinted in Soul on Ice. New York: Dell, 1970, pp. 97-111.

Coleman, John. "Second Opinion: Norman Mailer." Sunday Times Magazine (London), June 18, 1967, p. 34.

Cook, Bruce. "Norman Mailer: The Temptation to Power." Renascence, 14 (Summer, 1962), 206-15, 222.

_____. "Aquarius Rex." National Observer, November 4, 1972, pp. 1, 15. Reprinted in Will the Real Norman Mailer Please Stand Up?, ed. Laura Adams. Port Washington, New York: Kennikat Press, 1974. [See also St. George and the Godfather.]

Cooperman, Stanley. "The Devil's Advocate: Marching in Among the Saints." Chelsea 26: 156-66.

Corona, Mario. "Norman Mailer." Studi Americani, 11 (1965), 359-407.

Cowan, Michael. "The Americanness of Norman Mailer" in Norman Mailer: A Collection of Critical Essays, ed. Leo Braudy. Englewood Cliffs, New Jersey: Prentice-Hall, 1972,

pp. 143-51. Reprinted in Will the Real Norman
Mailer Please Stand Up?, ed. Laura Adams.
Port Washington, New York: Kennikat Press,
1974, pp. 95-111.

Cowley, Malcolm. "The Literary Situation, 1965."
University of Mississippi Quarterly, 6 (1965),
91-98.

Cunningham, Laura. "Prisoners of Mailer: Bea,
Adele, Lady Jean, Beverly, Carol, et al."
Cosmopolitan, January, 1973, pp. 104-09.

Davis, Robert Gorham. "Norman Mailer and the Trap
of Egotism." Story, 33 (Spring, 1960), 117-19.

DeMott, Benjamin. "Docket No. 15883." American
Scholar, 30 (Spring, 1961), 232-37.

Dienstfrey, Harris. "The Fiction of Norman Mailer"
in On Contemporary Literature, ed. Richard
Kostelanetz. New York: Hearst, 1964, pp. 422-
36.

Donohue, H. E. F. Conversations with Nelson Algren.
New York: Hill & Wang, 1964.

Drexler, Rosalyn. "What Happened to Mozart's Sister?"
Village Voice, May 6, 1971, p. 28.

Duhamel, P. Albert. "Love in the Modern Novel."
Catholic World, April, 1960, pp. 31-35.

The Editors. "Books by Norman Mailer." Hollins
Critic, 2 (June, 1965), 7.

Egginton, Joyce. "If I Become Mayor--by Norman
Mailer." Observer, May 11, 1969, p. 8.

Elliott, G. P. "Destroyers, Defilers, and Confusers
of Men." Atlantic, December, 1968, pp. 74-80.

Ellmann, Mary. "Phallic Criticism" in Thinking About

Women. New York: Harcourt Brace Jovanovich, 1968, pp. 11-163 passim. Reprinted in Women's Liberation and Literature, ed. Elaine Showalter. New York: Harcourt Brace Jovanovich, 1971, pp. 220-21.

Fenton, Charles A. "The Writers Who Came Out of the War." Saturday Review, August 3, 1957, pp. 5-7, 24.

Fiedler, Leslie A. "The Jew as Mythic American." Ramparts (Fall, 1963), 32-48.

_____. "The Breakthrough: The American Jewish Novelist and the Fictional Image of the Jew" in Recent American Fiction, ed. Joseph J. Waldmeir. Boston: Houghton Mifflin, 1963, pp. 84-109.

_____. Waiting for the End. New York: Dell, 1964, pp. 17-235 passim.

_____. "Caliban or Hamlet?" Encounter, April, 1966, pp. 23-27.

_____. Love and Death in the American Novel, rev. ed. New York: Dell, 1966, passim.

_____. "The End of the Novel" in Perspectives on Fiction, ed. James L. Calderwood and Harold E. Toliver. New York: Oxford University Press, 1968.

_____. The Return of the Vanishing American. New York: Stein and Day, 1968, pp. 14, 157.

_____. "The Male Novel." Partisan Review, 37 (1970), 74-89.

Finholt, Richard D. " 'Otherwise How Explain?' Norman Mailer's New Cosmology." Modern Fiction Studies, 17 (Autumn, 1971), 375-86. Reprinted in Will the Real Norman Mailer Please Stand Up?, ed. Laura Adams. Port Washington,

New York: Kennikat Press, 1974, pp. 80-94.

Finklestein, Sidney. "Norman Mailer and Edward
      Albee." American Dialog, 1 (October-November,
      1964), 23-28.

Fitch, R. E. "Mystique de la Merde." New Republic,
      September 3, 1956, pp. 17-18. [Reply: Time,
      October 1, 1956, p. 94.]

Flaherty, Joe. Managing Mailer. New York: Coward-
      McCann, 1969 [on mayoralty campaign].

_____. "The Mailer-Breslin Ticket: Vote the Ras-
      cals In." Village Voice, April 24, 1969, pp. 1,
      59.

Fleming, Thomas. "The Novelist as Journalist." New
      York Times Book Review, July 21, 1968, pp. 2,
      4.

Forsyth, R. A. " 'Europe,' 'Africa' and the Problem
      of Spiritual Authority." Southern Review, 3
      (1969), 294-323.

Foster, Richard. "Mailer and the Fitzgerald Tradition."
      Novel, 1 (Spring, 1968), 219-30. Reprinted in
      Norman Mailer: A Collection of Critical Essays,
      ed. Leo Braudy. Englewood Cliffs, New Jersey:
      Prentice-Hall, 1972, pp. 127-42.

_____. "Norman Mailer" in Seven American Liter-
      ary Stylists from Poe to Mailer: An Introduction,
      ed. George T. Wright. Minneapolis: University
      of Minnesota Press, 1973, pp. 238-73.

Fox, Tom. "Norman Mailer: The Fighting Man's
      Middle-aged Peacenik." Philadelphia Daily News,
      May 21, 1968, p. 4.

Galligan, Edward L. "Hemingway's Staying Power."
      Massachusetts Review, 8 (Summer, 1967), 431-39.

Gilman, Richard.   "Norman Mailer: Art as Life, Life
    as Art" in The Confusion of Realms.   New York:
    Random House, 1969, pp. 81-153.

Gindin, James.   "Megalotopia and the WASP Backlash:
    The Fiction of Mailer and Updike."   Critical
    Review, 15 (Winter, 1971), 38-52.

_____.   Harvest of a Quiet Eye: The Novel of Com-
    passion.   Bloomington: Indiana University Press,
    1971, pp. 352-57.

Girson, Rochelle.   " '48's Nine."   Saturday Review of
    Literature, February 12, 1949, p. 12.

Gittelson, Natalie.   "Norman Mailer: Devil in the
    Fire."   Harper's Bazaar, July, 1971, pp. 14, 16.

Glicksberg, Charles I.   "Sex in Contemporary Litera-
    ture."   Colorado Quarterly, 9 (Winter, 1961),
    277-87.

Goldman, Lawrence.   "The Political Vision of Norman
    Mailer."   Studies on the Left, 4 (Summer, 1964),
    129-41.

Goldstone, Herbert.   "The Novels of Norman Mailer."
    English Journal, 45 (March, 1956), 113-21.

Grace, Matthew.   "Norman Mailer at the End of the
    Decade."   Études Anglaises, 24 (January-March,
    1971), 50-58.   Reprinted in Will the Real Norman
    Mailer Please Stand Up?, ed. Laura Adams.
    Port Washington, New York: Kennikat Press,
    1974, pp. 10-22.

Grady, Sandy.   "Norman Mailer Raps Philly's Charity."
    Philadelphia Evening Bulletin, May 21, 1968,
    p. 61.

Graves, R.   "Norman Mailer at the Typewriter, Writing
    on the Moon Landing."   Life, August 29, 1969,
    p. 1.

Green, Martin. "Mailer and Amis: The New Conservatism." Nation (May 5, 1969), 573-75.

Greer, Germaine. "My Mailer Problem." Esquire, September, 1971, pp. 90-93, 214, 216.

Gross, Theodore L., ed. Representative Men: Cult Heroes of Our Time. New York: Free Press, 1970, pp. 212-16.

_____. "Norman Mailer: The Quest for Heroism" in The Heroic Ideal in American Literature. New York: Free Press, 1971, pp. 272-95.

_____, ed. The Literature of American Jews. Riverside, New Jersey: Free Press, 1973.

Guttmann, Allen. "Jewish Radicals, Jewish Writers." American Scholar, 32 (Autumn, 1963), 563-75.

_____. "The Conversion of the Jews." Wisconsin Studies in Contemporary Literature, 6 (Summer, 1965), 161-76.

_____. The Jewish Writer in America: Assimilation and the Crisis of Identity. New York: Oxford University Press, 1971.

_____. "Norman Mailer: The Writer as Radical" in Amerikanische Literatur im 20. Jahrhundert/ American Literature in the 20th Century, eds. Alfred Weber and Dietmar Haack. Göttingen: Vandenhoeck & Ruprecht, 1971, pp. 92-106 [Summary in German, pp. 104-06].

"A Half Century of Mailer." Newsweek, February 19, 1973, p. 78.

Harper, Howard M., Jr. Desperate Faith: A Study of Bellow, Salinger, Mailer, Baldwin and Updike. Chapel Hill: University of North Carolina Press, 1967, pp. 96-136.

Hassan, Ihab. <u>Radical Innocence: Studies in the Con-temporary American Novel</u>. New York: Harper & Row, 1961, pp. 140-51 et passim.

_____. "The Way Down and Out: Spiritual Deflec-tion in Recent American Fiction." <u>Virginia Quar-terly Review</u>, 39 (Winter, 1963), 81-93.

_____. "The Novel of Outrage: A Minority Voice in Postwar American Fiction." <u>American Scholar</u>, 35 (1965), 239-53 passim.

_____. <u>Contemporary American Literature, 1945-1972: An Introduction</u>. New York: Frederick Ungar, 1973, pp. 31-36 et passim.

Healey, Robert C. "Novelists of the War: A Bunch of Dispossessed" in <u>Fifty Years of the American Novel</u>, ed. Harold C. Gardiner. New York: Scribner's, 1951, pp. 251-71.

Helsa, David. "The Two Roles of Norman Mailer" in <u>Adversity and Grace</u>, ed. Nathan A. Scott. Chicago: University of Chicago Press, 1968, pp. 211-38.

Hentoff, Nat. "Behold the New Journalism--It's Coming After You!" <u>Evergreen Review</u>, July, 1968, pp. 49-51.

Hicks, Granville. "They Needn't Say No." <u>Saturday Review</u>, July 2, 1960, p. 14.

_____. "Norman Mailer: Foreword" in <u>Literary Horizons: A Quarter Century of American Fic-tion</u>. New York: New York University Press, 1970, pp. 273-74.

Hoffman, Frederick J. "Norman Mailer and the Revolt of the Ego: Some Observations in Recent Ameri-can Literature." <u>Wisconsin Studies in Contem-porary Literature</u>, 1 (Fall, 1960), 5-12. Reprinted

as "Norman Mailer e la Rivolta dell'Io." Il
Tempo di Letteratura, 1 (1963), 201-09.

_____. The Modern Novel in America. Chicago:
Henry Regnery, 1963, pp. xi-xii, 193, 195, 233,
251-52.

_____. The Mortal No: Death and the Modern
Imagination. Princeton: Princeton University
Press, 1964, pp. 210-492 passim.

Holland, Michael. "How to Crack Esquire." Esquire,
December, 1964, p. 90.

Hope, Francis. "Hunting Trip." New Statesman, 77
(April 4, 1969), 485-86.

"In the Money." People, March 11, 1974, p. 22.

Iwamoto, Iwao. "Gendai wo Ikiru Messiah." Eigo
Seinen, 115 (1969), 554-55.

Johnson, Michael L. The New Journalism: The Under-
ground Press, The Artists of Nonfiction, and
Changes in the Established Media. Lawrence:
University Press of Kansas, 1971, pp. 64-84 et
passim. Reprinted in Will the Real Norman
Mailer Please Stand Up?, ed. Laura Adams,
Port Washington, New York: Kennikat Press,
1974, pp. 173-94.

Jones, James. "Small Comment from a Penitent
Novelist." Esquire, December, 1963, pp. 40-44.

Kahn, E. J. "When the Real Norman Mailer Stands
Up, Please Don't Lay a Hand on Me." Holiday,
March, 1968, pp. 34, 36, 37.

Kaufmann, Donald. "The Long Happy Life of Norman
Mailer." Modern Fiction Studies, 17 (Autumn,
1971), 347-49.

Kazin, Alfred. "The Alone Generation: A Comment on

the Fiction of the 'Fifties.' " Harper's, October,
1959, pp. 127-31.

_____. "The Jew as Modern Writer." Commentary,
April, 1966, pp. 37-41.

_____. "Imagination and the Age." Reporter,
May 5, 1966, pp. 32-35.

_____. "The Literary Sixties, When the World Was
Too Much With Us." New York Times Book Review, December 21, 1969, pp. 1-3, 18.

_____. "The War Novel: From Mailer to Vonnegut."
Saturday Review, February 6, 1971, pp. 13-15,
36. Reprinted in Bright Book of Life: American
Novelists and Storytellers from Hemingway to
Mailer. Boston: Little, Brown, 1973.

_____. "The World as a Novel: From Capote to
Mailer." New York Review of Books, April 18,
1971, pp. 26-30.

_____. "New York Jew." New York Review of
Books, December 14, 1972, pp. 4, 6, 8, 10, 11.

_____. Bright Book of Life: American Novelists
and Storytellers from Hemingway to Mailer.
Boston: Little, Brown, 1973, pp. 71-77, 149-57,
236-41, 255-57 et passim.

Kelly, Sean. "Norman the Barbarian." National
Lampoon, May, 1972, pp. 33-37.

Kermode, Frank. "World Without End or Beginning."
Malahat Review, 1 (1967), 113-29.

Krim, Seymour. "Norman Mailer, Get Out of My
Head!" New York, April 21, 1969, pp. 35-42.

Kunitz, Stanley J. Twentieth Century Authors, First
Supplement. New York: H. W. Wilson, 1955,
pp. 628-29.

Kyria, Pierre. "Regards sur la Littérature Ameri-
    caine." Revue de Paris, March, 1968, pp. 117-
    22.

Lakin, R. D. "The Misplaced Writer in America."
    Midwest Quarterly, 4 (Summer, 1963), 295-303.

Land, Myrick. "Mr. Norman Mailer Challenges All
    the Talent in the Room" in The Fine Art of
    Literary Mayhem. New York: Holt, Rinehart &
    Winston, 1963, pp. 216-38.

Langbaum, Robert. "Mailer's New Style." Novel, 2
    (Fall, 1968) 69-78. Reprinted in The Modern
    Spirit. New York: Oxford University Press,
    1970, pp. 147-63.

Lasch, Christopher. The New Radicalism in America
    [1889-1963]: The Intellectual as a Social Type.
    New York: Knopf, 1966, pp. 334-49.

Leffelaar, H. L. "Norman Mailer in Chicago."
    Litterair Paspoort, November, 1959, pp. 79-81.

Lehan, Richard. "The Outer Limits: Norman Mailer
    and Richard Wright" in A Dangerous Crossing:
    French Literary Existentialism and the Modern
    American Novel. Carbondale and Edwardsville:
    Southern Illinois University Press, 1973, pp. 80-
    95.

Lelchuk, Alan. American Mischief. New York:
    Farrar, Straus & Giroux, 1973, pp. 279-97 et
    passim.

Leonard, John. "Happy Birthday, Norman Mailer."
    New York Times Book Review, February 18,
    1973, p. 35.

Levine, Paul. "The Intemperate Zone: The Climate
    of Contemporary American Fiction." Massachu-
    setts Review, 8 (Summer, 1967), 505-23.

Levine, Richard M. "When Sam and Sergius Meet."
New Leader, July 8, 1968, pp. 16-19. Reprinted
in Will the Real Norman Mailer Please Stand Up?,
ed. Laura Adams. Port Washington, New York:
Kennikat Press, 1974, pp. 23-33.

Lewis, R. W. B. "Recent Fiction: Picaro and Pil-
grim" in A Time of Harvest: American Literature 1910-1960, ed. Robert E. Spiller. New
York: Hill & Wang, 1962, pp. 144-53.

Lingeman, Richard R. "The Last Word: Writers as
Show-Biz." New York Times Book Review,
July 25, 1971, p. 27.

Lodge, David. "The Novelist at the Crossroads."
Critical Quarterly, 11 (Summer, 1969), 105-32.
Reprinted in The Novelist at the Crossroads,
And Other Essays on Fiction and Criticism.
Ithaca: Cornell University Press, 1971, pp. 10-
12 et passim.

Lowell, Robert. Notebook: 1967-68. New York:
Farrar, Straus & Giroux, 1969, p. 108; 3rd
edition, 1970, p. 183.

Lucid, Robert F. "Introduction" in The Long Patrol:
25 Years of Writing from the Work of Norman
Mailer, ed. Robert F. Lucid. New York: World,
1971, pp. xi-xxvii. [Lucid also introduces each
selection.]

_____. "Introduction" in Norman Mailer: The Man
and His Work, ed. Robert F. Lucid. Boston:
Little, Brown, 1971, pp. 1-18.

_____. "F. Scott Fitzgerald, Ernest Hemingway and
Norman Mailer: Three Public Performances."
American Scholar (Summer, 1974).

Ludwig, Jack. Recent American Novelists (University
of Minnesota Pamphlets on American Writers).

Minneapolis: University of Minnesota Press,
1962, pp. 24-28.

Lundkvist, Artur. "Ordspruta och gentlemann agangster:
Norman Mailer" in Utflykter Ned Utlandska For-
fattare. Stockholm: Bonniers, 1969, pp. 155-69.

Macdonald, Dwight. "The Bright Young Men in the
Arts." Esquire, September, 1958, pp. 38-40.

_____. "Our Far-flung Correspondents: Massachu-
setts vs. Mailer." New Yorker, October 8, 1960,
pp. 154-56, 58, 60-66. Reprinted in Norman
Mailer: The Man and His Work, ed. Robert F.
Lucid. Boston: Little, Brown, 1971, pp. 203-17.

Madden, David, ed. American Dreams, American
Nightmares. Carbondale: Southern Illinois University Press, 1970, pp. xli-xlii.

Maddison, Michael. "Prospect of Commitment."
Political Quarterly (October, 1961), 353-62.

"Mailer for Mayor." Time, June 13, 1969, pp. 21-22.

"The Mailer Problem." Spectator (May 1, 1964), 598.

Malin, Irving and Irwin Stark, eds. Breakthrough: A
Treasury of Contemporary American-Jewish
Literature. New York: McGraw-Hill, 1964,
pp. 1-24.

Malin, Irving. Jews and Americans. Carbondale:
Southern Illinois University Press, 1965.

_____, ed. Contemporary American-Jewish Litera-
ture: Critical Essays. Bloomington: Indiana
University Press, 1973.

Maloff, Saul. "Mailer on the High Wire." Commonweal (June 30, 1972), 361-63.

Mano, D. Keith. "Mailer Bombs." National Review,

25 (March 16, 1973), 315-16.

Manso, Peter, ed. Running Against the Machine. Garden City, New York: Doubleday, 1969 [on mayoralty campaign].

Martien, Norman. "Norman Mailer at Graduate School: One Man's Effort." New American Review #1, pp. 233-41. Reprinted in Norman Mailer: The Man and His Work, ed. Robert F. Lucid. Boston: Little, Brown, 1971, pp. 245-55.

Marx, Leo. "Noble Shit": The Uncivil Response of American Writers to Civil Religion in America." Massachusetts Review (Autumn, 1973), 709-39.

Materassi, Mario. "La Rauca Voce di Norman Mailer." Ponte, 23 (1967), 630-35.

Miller, Wayne Charles. An Armed America: Its Face in Fiction. New York: New York University Press, 1970, pp. 158-62.

Millett, Kate. Sexual Politics. Garden City: Doubleday, 1970, pp. 314-35.

Millgate, Michael. American Social Fiction: James to Cozzens. New York: Barnes and Noble, 1964, pp. 146-50, 159-64.

Morton, Fredric. "Sexism--A Better Show than Sex." Village Voice, May 6, 1971, pp. 70, 72, 75.

Mudrick, Marvin. "Mailer and Styron: Guests of the Establishment." Hudson Review, 17 (Autumn, 1964), 346-66. Reprinted as "Mailer and Styron" in On Culture and Literature. New York: Horizon, 1970, pp. 176-99.

Muste, John M. "Norman Mailer and John Dos Passos: The Question of Influence." Modern Fiction Studies, 17 (Autumn, 1971), 361-74.

"Mystique de la Merde." Time, October 1, 1956,
     p. 94. [cf. Robert E. Fitch. "Mystique de la
     Merde." New Republic, September 3, 1956,
     pp. 17-18.]

Nedelin, V. "War Lovers and Their Victims." Ino-
     strannaja Literatura [Foreign Literature], 7
     (July, 1961), 171-84.

Newfield, Jack. "On the Steps of a Zeitgeist" in Bread
     and Roses Too. New York: E. P. Dutton, 1971,
     pp. 385-90.

_____. "Is There a 'New Journalism'?" Columbia
     Journalism Review, July-August, 1972, pp. 45-47.

Newman, Paul B. "Mailer: The Jew as Existentialist."
     North American Review, 2 (1965), 48-55.

New York Times, March 17, 1974, p. 33.

Nobile, Philip. "A Review of the New York Review of
     Books." Esquire, April, 1972, pp. 103-26.

Noble, David W. The Eternal Adam and the New World
     Garden: The Central Myth in the American Novel
     Since 1830. New York: George Braziller, 1968,
     pp. 197-209.

Normand, J. "L'homme mystifié: Les héros de
     Bellow, Albee, Styron et Mailer." Études
     Anglaises, 72 (1969), 370-85.

"Notre Dame Meets Norman Mailer." Panorama,
     April 6, 1968, pp. 3ff.

"Odd Couple." Newsweek, May 12, 1969, pp. 37-38.

Ostriker, Dane Proxpeale. "Norman Mailer and the
     Mystery Woman or, The Rape of the C--k."
     Esquire, November, 1972, pp. 122-25.

Pace, Eric. "Mailer Rants Over Book on Mailer Shot

in Rear." Dayton Daily News, October 19, 1972, p. 63.

Peter, John. "The Self-effacement of the Novelist." Malahat Review, 8 (October, 1968), 119-28.

Pfeil, Sigmar. "Bemerkungen zu einigen Bedeutanden amerikanischen Kriegsromanen über den 2 Weltkrieg." Zeitschrift für Anglistik und Amerikanistik, 13 (1965), 61-74.

Phillips, William. "Writing about Sex." Partisan Review, 24 (Fall, 1967), 552-63 passim.

Pilati, J. "On the Steps of City Hall." Commonweal (May 16, 1969), 255-56.

Podhoretz, Norman. "Norman Mailer: The Embattled Vision." Partisan Review (Summer, 1959), 371-91. Reprinted as introduction to Barbary Shore. New York: Grosset Universal Library; in Recent American Fiction, ed. Joseph J. Waldmeir. Boston: Houghton Mifflin, 1963, pp. 185-202; in Doings and Undoings. New York: Farrar, Straus & Giroux, 1959; and in Norman Mailer: The Man and His Work, ed. Robert F. Lucid. Boston: Little, Brown, 1971, pp. 60-85.

_____. Making It. New York: Random House, 1967, pp. 352-56.

Poirier, Richard. The Performing Self. New York: Oxford University Press, 1971, pp. 5-181 passim.

_____. "Minority Within." Partisan Review, 39 (1972), 12-43.

_____. "Mailer: Good Form and Bad." Saturday Review, April 22, 1972, pp. 42-46. Reprinted in Will the Real Norman Mailer Please Stand Up?, ed. Laura Adams. Port Washington, New York: Kennikat Press, 1974.

_____. "Norman Mailer: A Self-creation." Atlantic, October, 1972, pp. 78-85.

_____. "Norman Mailer's Necessary Mess." Listener, 90 (November 8, 1973), 626-27.

Popescu, Petru. "Norman Mailer: Cei goi si cei morti." Romania Literara, February 6, 1968, p. 19.

"PPA Press Conference." Publishers' Weekly, March 22, 1965, pp. 30-31, 41-45.

Prescott, Orville. "Novelists and The War" in In My Opinion: An Inquiry into the Contemporary Novel. New York: Bobbs-Merrill, 1952, pp. 146-64.

Quinn, Sally. "Norman Mailer Turns 50." Washington Post, February 7, 1973, pp. B1, B7.

Raes, Hugo. "Nieuw Vooruitstrevend Amerikaans Proza." De Vlaamse Gids, 45 (November, 1961), 751-56.

Rambures, Jean-Louis de. "Norman Mailer: l'Enfant Terrible des Lettres Americaines." Realités, June, 1968, pp. 95-105.

Rawson, C. J. "Catalogues, Corpses, and Cannibals: Swift and Mailer with Reflections on Whitman, Conrad and Others" in Gulliver and the Gentle Reader. London: Routledge and Kegan Paul, 1973, pp. 100-52 et passim.

Raymont, Henry. "National Book Awards: The Winners." New York Times, March 11, 1969, p. 42.

Reeves, Richard. "Mailer and Breslin Enter Race." New York Times, May 2, 1969, p. 24.

"The Reporter." Observer, August 17, 1969, p. 7.

Rijpens, John. "Mailer Weer op Oorlogspad." De

Vlaamse Gids, 52 (1968), 27-29.

Robinson, Leonard W. "The New Journalism."
Writer's Digest, January, 1970, pp. 32-35, 19.

Rodman, Seldon. "Norman Mailer" in Tongues of
Fallen Angels. New York: New Directions,
1974, pp. 163-81.

Rosenbaum, Ron. "The Siege of Mailer: Hero to His-
torian." Village Voice, January 21, 1971, pp. 1,
38, 40-42, 48.

Rosenthal, T. G. "The Death of Fiction." New Statesman (March 22, 1968), 389.

Ross, Frank. "The Assailant-victim in Three War-
protest Novels." Paunch, 32 (August, 1968),
46-57.

Ross, Morton L. "Thoreau and Mailer: The Mission
of the Rooster." Western Humanities Review, 25
(Winter, 1971), 47-56.

Rothe, Anna, ed. Current Biography, 1948. New
York: H. W. Wilson, 1949, pp. 408-10.

Rubin, Louis D. , Jr. "The Curious Death of the Novel:
Or, What to Do About Tired Literary Critics."
Kenyon Review, 28 (1966), 305-25. Reprinted in
The Curious Death of the Novel: Essays in Amer-
ican Literature. Baton Rouge: Louisiana State
University Press, 1967, pp. 3-23.

Sadoya, Shigenobu. "Norman Mailer's Existentialism."
Studies in English Language and Literature,
(Seinan Gakuin University, Japan), July, 1963,
pp. 39-58 [in Japanese].

_____. "Norman Mailer: An Introduction." Studies
of American Novels: Norman Mailer Number
(Seinan Gakuin University, Japan), 1 (May 25,
1973).

"Savage Ending." Newsweek, December 5, 1960, p. 33.

Sayre, Nora. "Happy Days Are Here Again: The
    Guest Word." New York Times Book Review,
    October 22, 1972, p. 55.

Schein, H. "Norman Mailer." Bonniers Litterara
    Magasin, 26 (March, 1957), 232-40.

Schrader, George A. "Norman Mailer and the Despair
    of Defiance." Yale Review, 51 (December, 1961),
    267-80. Reprinted in Norman Mailer: A Collec-
    tion of Critical Essays, ed. Leo Braudy. Engle-
    wood Cliffs, New Jersey: Prentice-Hall, 1972,
    pp. 82-95.

_____. "Norman Mailer." America (November 30,
    1968), 558.

Schroth, Raymond A. "Mailer and His Gods." Com-
    monweal, 90 (May 9, 1969), 226-29. Reprinted
    in Will the Real Norman Mailer Please Stand Up?,
    ed. Laura Adams. Port Washington, New York:
    Kennikat Press, 1974, pp. 34-42.

Schulz, Max F. "Mailer's Divine Comedy." Wisconsin
    Studies in Contemporary Literature, 9 (Winter,
    1968), 36-57. Reprinted in Radical Sophistication:
    Studies in Contemporary Jewish-American
    Novelists. Athens: Ohio University Press, 1969,
    pp. 69-109; and in Will the Real Norman Mailer
    Please Stand Up?, ed. Laura Adams. Port Washing-
    ton, New York: Kennikat Press, 1974, pp. 43-79.

_____. Contemporary Literature, 13 (Spring, 1972),
    243-48.

Scott, Nathan A., Jr. Three American Novelists--
    Mailer, Bellow, Trilling. South Bend: Notre
    Dame University Press, 1973.

Shaw, Peter. "The Tough Guy Intellectual." Critical
    Quarterly, 8 (Spring, 1966), 13-28.

Sheed, Wilfred. "Norman Mailer: Genius or Nothing."
Encounter, June, 1971, pp. 66-71. Reprinted in
The Morning After. New York: Farrar, Straus
& Giroux, 1971, pp. 9-17.

Smith, Henry Nash. "The American Scholar Today."
Southwest Review, 48 (1963), 191-99.

Sokolov, Raymond A. "Flying High with Mailer."
Newsweek, December 9, 1968, pp. 84, 86-88.

Solotaroff, Robert. "Down Mailer's Way." Chicago
Review, 19 (June, 1967), 11-25.

Stern, Daniel. "The Mysterious New Novel" in Libera-
tions: New Essays on the Humanities in Revolution, ed. Ihab Hassan. Middletown, Connecticut:
Wesleyan University Press, 1971, pp. 30, 33 et
passim.

Stern, Richard. "Report from the MLA." New York
Review of Books, February 17, 1966, pp. 26-28.

Stevenson, David L. "Fiction's Unfamiliar Face."
Nation, 187 (November 1, 1958), 307-09.

_____. "Stryon and the Fiction of the Fifties."
Critique, 3 (Summer, 1960), 47-58.

Styron, William. "On Our Literature of Collision."
Intellectual Digest, March, 1972, pp. 82-84.

Tanner, Tony. "On the Parapet" in City of Words:
American Fiction 1950-1970. New York: Harper
& Row, 1971, pp. 348-71. Reprinted in Will the
Real Norman Mailer Please Stand Up?, ed.,
Laura Adams. Port Washington, New York:
Kennikat Press, 1974, pp. 113-49.

Taylor, Gordon O. "Of Adams and Aquarius." American Literature, 46 (March, 1974), 68-72.

Taylor, Robert, Jr. "Sounding the Trumpets of

Defiance: Mark Twain and Norman Mailer."
Mark Twain Journal, 16 (Winter, 1972), 1-14.

Thorp, Willard. American Writing in the Twentieth
    Century. Cambridge: Harvard University Press,
    1960, pp. 136-47 passim.

"Tilting at Politics." Economist, June 14, 1969, p. 48.

Toback, James. "Norman Mailer Today." Commen-
    tary, October, 1967, pp. 68-76.

_____. "At Play in the Fields of the Bored."
    Esquire, December, 1968, pp. 150-55, 22, 24,
    26, 28, 30, 32, 34, 36.

Trilling, Diana. "Norman Mailer." Encounter, No-
    vember, 1962, pp. 45-56. Reprinted as "The
    Moral Radicalism of Norman Mailer" in Clare-
    mont Essays. New York: Harcourt Brace &
    World, 1962, pp. 175-202; in The Creative
    Present, ed. Nona Balakian and Charles Simmons.
    Garden City, New York: Doubleday, 1963,
    pp. 145-71; in Norman Mailer: The Man and
    His Work, ed. Robert F. Lucid. Boston: Little,
    Brown, 1971, pp. 108-36; and in Norman Mailer:
    A Collection of Critical Essays, ed. Leo Braudy.
    Englewood Cliffs, New Jersey: Prentice-Hall,
    1972, pp. 42-65.

Volpe, Edmund L. "James Jones--Norman Mailer" in
    Contemporary American Novelists, ed. Harry T.
    Moore. Carbondale: Southern Illinois University
    Press, 1964, pp. 106-19.

Wagenheim, Allan J. "Is It Time for an Epigraph?
    Notes on Modern Essay." Denver Quarterly, 3
    (Winter, 1969), 85-90.

Waldmeir, Joseph J. "Accommodation in the New
    Novel." University College Quarterly, 11
    (November, 1965), 26-32.

_____. "Only an Occasional Rutabaga: American Fiction Since 1945." Modern Fiction Studies, 15 (Winter, 1969-70), 467-81.

Weinberg, Helen. "The Heroes of Norman Mailer's Novels" in The New Novel in America: The Kafkan Mode in Contemporary Fiction. Ithaca: Cornell University Press, 1970, pp. 108-40 et passim.

_____. "The Activist Norman Mailer" in Contemporary American Jewish Literature: Critical Essays, ed. Irving Malin. Bloomington: Indiana University Press, 1973.

Weinraub, Bernard. "Mailer the Author Will Donate Prize to Mailer the Politician." New York Times, May 6, 1969, p. 35.

Widmar, Kingsley. "The Hollywood Image." Coastlines, 5 (Autumn, 1961), 17-27.

_____. "Several American Perplexes" in The Literary Rebel. Carbondale: Southern Illinois University Press, 1965, pp. 18-243 passim.

Willingham, Calder. "The Way It Isn't Done: Notes on the Distress of Norman Mailer." Esquire, December, 1963, pp. 306-08. Reprinted in Norman Mailer: The Man and His Work, ed. Robert F. Lucid. Boston: Little, Brown, 1971, pp. 238-44.

Wilson, Robert Anton. "Negative Thinking: the New Art of the Brave." Realist, December, 1960, pp. 5, 11-13.

_____. "An Open Letter to Norman Mailer." Way Out (Journal of The School of Living, Brookville, Ohio), February, 1963, pp. 50-57.

Winegarten, Renee. "Norman Mailer--Genuine or Counterfeit?" Midstream, 11 (September, 1965), 91-95.

Winn, Janet. "Capote, Mailer and Miss Parker." New Republic, February 9, 1959, pp. 27-28.

Witt, Grace. "The Bad Man as Hipster: Norman Mailer's Use of the Frontier Metaphor." Western American Literature, 4 (Fall, 1969), 203-17.

Wolfe, Tom. "The New Journalism" in The New Journalism, ed. Tom Wolfe and E. W. Johnson. New York: Harper and Row, 1973, pp. 27-28 et passim.

Wood, Margery. "Norman Mailer and Nathalie Sarraute: A Comparison of Existential Novels." Minnesota Review, 6 (1966), 67-72.

Woodley, R. "Literary Ticket for the 51st State." Life, May 30, 1969, pp. 71-72.

Woodress, James. "The Anatomy of Recent Fiction Reviewing." Midwest Quarterly, 2 (Autumn, 1960), 67-81.

Wright, George T. , ed. Seven American Literary Stylists from Poe to Mailer: An Introduction. Minneapolis: University of Minnesota Press, 1973.

Wüstenhagen, Heinz. "Instinkt Kontra Vernunft: Norman Mailers ideologische und aesthetische Konfusion." Zeitschrift für Anglistik und Amerikanistik, 16 (1968), 362-89.

Yamamoto, H. "The Realistic Consciousness of Norman Mailer." American Literature Review (Tokyo), April, 1961, pp. 10-11 [in Japanese].

E. BOOKS ON MAILER

1. FULL-LENGTH STUDIES

Kaufmann, Donald L. Norman Mailer: The Countdown/
    The First Twenty Years. Carbondale: Southern
    Illinois University Press, 1969.

Leeds, Barry H. The Structured Vision of Norman
    Mailer. New York: New York University Press,
    1969.

Nojima, Hidekatsu. Norman Mailer. Tokyo:
    Kenkyusha, 1971. [In Japanese].

Poirier, Richard. Norman Mailer (Modern Masters
    Series). New York: Viking Press, 1972.

Solotaroff, Robert. Down Mailer's Way. Urbana:
    University of Illinois Press, 1974.

2. MONOGRAPHS

Bufithis, Philip H. Norman Mailer. New York:
    Frederick Ungar, 1974.

Foster, Richard J. Norman Mailer (University of
    Minnesota Pamphlets on American Writers).
    Minneapolis: University of Minnesota Press,
    1968. Reprinted in Norman Mailer: The Man
    and His Work, ed. Robert F. Lucid. Boston:
    Little, Brown, 1971, pp. 21-59.

Sadoya, Shigenobu, ed. The Studies of American
    Novels: Norman Mailer Number (Seinan Gakuin
    University, Japan), 1 (May 25, 1973).

"Studies of Norman Mailer." Modern Fiction Studies,
    17 (Autumn, 1971), 347-463.

3.   CRITICAL COLLECTIONS

Adams, Laura, ed. Will the Real Norman Mailer
    Please Stand Up? Port Washington, New York:
    Kennikat Press, 1974.
        Contents:
        Laura Adams.   "Introduction"
        Matthew Grace.   "Norman Mailer at the End
            of the Decade"
        Richard A. Schroth.   "Mailer and His Gods"
        Max F. Schulz.   "Norman Mailer's Divine
            Comedy"
        Richard D. Finholt.   "Otherwise How Explain?
            Norman Mailer's New Cosmology"
        Michael Cowan.   "The Americanness of Norman
            Mailer"
        Tony Tanner.   "On the Parapet"
        Barry H. Leeds.   "Deaths for the Ladies, and
            Other Disasters"
        Gerald Weales.   "The Park in the Playhouse"
        Leo Braudy.   "Maidstone: A Mystery"
        Michael L. Johnson.   "Norman Mailer"
        Jane O'Reilly.   "Diary of a Mailer Trailer"
        Joyce Carol Oates.   "Out of the Machine"
        Bruce Cook.   "Aquarius Rex"
        Richard Poirier.   "Mailer: Good Form and
            Bad"
        Notes on the Editor and Contributors
        Bibliography

Braudy, Leo, ed. Norman Mailer: A Collection of
    Critical Essays (Twentieth Century Interpretations).
    Englewood Cliffs, New Jersey: Prentice-Hall,
    1972.
        Contents:

Leo Braudy. Introduction: "Norman Mailer: The Pride of Vulnerability"

Steven Marcus. "An Interview with Norman Mailer"

Diana Trilling. "The Radical Moralism of Norman Mailer"

James Baldwin. "The Black Boy Looks at the White Boy"

George Alfred Schrader. "Norman Mailer and the Despair of Defiance"

F. W. Dupee. "The American Norman Mailer"

Stanley Edgar Hyman. "Norman Mailer's Yummy Rump"

John W. Aldridge. "The Energy of New Success"

Leo Bersani. "Interpretation of Dreams"

Richard Foster. "Mailer and the Fitzgerald Tradition"

Michael Cowan. "The Americanness of Norman Mailer"

Richard Gilman. "What Mailer Has Done"

Richard Poirier. "The Ups and Down of Mailer"

Chronology of Important Dates

Notes on the Editor and Contributors

Selected Bibliography

Lucid, Robert F., ed. <u>Norman Mailer: The Man and His Work</u>. Boston: Little, Brown, 1971.

Contents:

Robert F. Lucid. "Introduction"

Richard Foster. "Norman Mailer"

Norman Podhoretz. "Norman Mailer: The Embattled Vision"

Alfred Kazin. "How Good Is Norman Mailer?"

Gore Vidal. "Norman Mailer" The Angels Are White"

Diana Trilling. "The Moral Radicalism of Norman Mailer"

Midge Decter. "Mailer's Campaign"

Elizabeth Hardwick. "A Nightmare by Norman Mailer"

Tom Wolfe. "Son of Crime and Punishment"

F. THESES AND DISSERTATIONS

1. THESES

Altherr, Thomas. M. A. Thesis, Ohio State University, 1973.

Bertrand, Suzanne. "Norman Mailer as a Novelist." M. A. Thesis, University of Montreal, 1962.

Cook, William J. "Norman Mailer's American Dream." M. A. Thesis, University of Alberta, 1967.

Dabney, Richard Lawson. "Norman Mailer's Hipster." M. A. Thesis, The American University, 1969.

Toback, James. M. A. Thesis, Columbia University, 1966.

2. DISSERTATIONS

Adams, Laura. "Norman Mailer's Aesthetics of Growth." Diss. McMaster University (Canada), 1972.

Baumbach, Jonathan. "The Theme of Guilt and Redemption in the Post-Second World War American Novel." Diss. Stanford University, 1961.

Bronson, Daniel Ross. "In Pursuit of the Elusive Present: The Poetry and Prose of Norman Mailer." Diss. University of Pennsylvania, 1972.

Bufithis, Philip H. "The Artist's Fight for Art: The
    Psychiatrist Figure in the Fiction of Major Con-
    temporary American Novelists." Diss. University
    of Pennsylvania, 1971.

Dabney, Richard Lawson. "The Rebel and the Hipster
    [Mailer and Camus]." Diss. George Washington
    University, 1971.

Fendelman, Earl B. "Toward a Third Voice: Auto-
    biographical Form in Thoreau, Stein, Adams, and
    Mailer." Diss. Yale University, 1971.

Ferreira, James Manuel. "The Radical Individualism
    of Norman Mailer." Diss. University of Minne-
    sota, 1972.

Flint, Joyce Marlene. "In Search of Meaning: Bernard
    Malamud, Norman Mailer, John Updike." Diss.
    Washington State University, 1969, pp. 5-146 pas-
    sim.

Gutman, Stanley T. "Mankind in Barbary: The Indi-
    vidual and Society in the Novels of Norman
    Mailer." Diss. Duke University, 1971.

Harper, Howard M. "Concepts of Human Destiny in
    Five American Novelists: Bellow, Salinger,
    Mailer, Baldwin, Updike." Diss. University of
    Pennsylvania, 1964.

Hux, Samuel Holland. "American Myth and Existential
    Vision: The Indigenous Existentialism of Mailer,
    Bellow, Styron and Ellison." Diss. University of
    Connecticut, 1965, pp. 179-211.

Kaufmann, Donald L. "Norman Mailer from 1948 to
    1963: The Sixth Mission." Diss. University of
    Iowa, 1967.

Kilgo, James P. "Five American Novels of World War
    II: A Critical Study." Diss. Tulane, 1971.

Klein, Marcus N.   "The Novel in America in the
1950's: An Introduction to a Thematic Study."
Diss. Columbia University, 1962.

Lawler, Robert W.   "Norman Mailer: The Connection
of New Circuits."   Diss. Claremont Graduate
School, 1969.

Lee, Lynn Allen.   "The Significant Popular Novel as
American Literature, 1920-1930;   1950-1960."
Diss. University of Minnesota, 1968, pp. 175-
232.

Leeds, Barry H.   "An Architecture to Eternity: The
Structured Vision of Norman Mailer's Fiction."
Diss. Ohio University.

Lucid, Luellen.   "The Writer as Public Figure: Mailer,
Sartre, Solzhenitsyn: An Essay in the Sociology
of Literature."   Diss. Yale University, 1973.

Merrill, Robert Wright.   "A Fondness for Order: The
Achievement of Norman Mailer."   Diss. University
of Chicago, 1972.

Nadon, Robert J.   "Urban Values in Recent American
Fiction: A Study of the City in the Fiction of
Saul Bellow, John Updike, Philip Roth, Bernard
Malamud, and Norman Mailer."   Diss. University
of Minnesota, 1969.

Rosenthal, Melvin.   "The American Writer and His
Society: The Response to Estrangement in the
Words of Nathaniel Hawthorne, Randolph Bourne,
Edmund Wilson, Norman Mailer, Saul Bellow."
Diss. University of Connecticut, 1970.

Scott, James B.   "The Individual and Society: Norman
Mailer Versus William Styron."   Diss. Syracuse
University, 1964.

Sheridan, James J.   "Form and Matter in Norman

Mailer." Diss. Case Western Reserve University, 1973.

Silverstein, Howard. "Norman Mailer and the Quest for Manhood." Diss. New York University, 1972.

Smith, Marcus A. J. "The Art and Influence of Nathanael West." Dissertation Abstracts, 25 (1965), 4155-56.

Solotaroff, Robert D. "Growth and the Open Future in the Writings of Norman Mailer." Diss. University of Chicago, 1970.

Spicehandler, Daniel. "The American War Novel." Diss. Columbia University, 1960, pp. 200-03.

Stark, John Olsen. "Norman Mailer's Works from 1963 to 1968." Diss. University of Wisconsin, 1970.

Wiener, David Morris. "The Politics of Love: Norman Mailer's Existential Vision." Diss. Syracuse University, 1972.

3.   RESEARCH IN PROGRESS

Finholt, Ronald. Diss. Northern Illinois University.

Holmes, Carol. [A variorum edition of The Deer Park]. Diss. State University of New York at Buffalo.

Lennon, Michael. "The Non-Fiction of Norman Mailer: Third Person Personal." Diss. University of Rhode Island [expected completion: fall, 1974].

Unger, Pamela. "Searching for a Style: The Literary Development of Norman Mailer." Diss. Ohio State University [expected completion: August, 1974].

G.   UNPUBLISHED WORK

Adams, Laura.   Norman Mailer's Aesthetics of Growth.
Book.   Forthcoming in 1975 from Ohio University
Press.

Crowther, Frank.   Chapter on Mailer in Give Me a Ticket
To Wherever It Is: A Slightly Fictional Memoir.

Grace, Matthew.   Essay on Mailer for a critical anthology on American novelists to be published in
1975 by Everett-Edwards.

Lucid, Robert.   Article on "The growing tendency to
express necrophile hostility" to Mailer.

H.   INTERVIEWS

Auchincloss, Eve and Nancy Lynch.   "An Interview
with Norman Mailer."   Mademoiselle, February,
1961, pp. 76, 160-63.

Bragg, Melvyn.   "The Bizarre Business of Writing a
Hypothetical Life of Marilyn Monroe."   Listener,
90 (December 20, 1973), pp. 847-50.

Breit, Harvey.   "Talk with Norman Mailer."   New
York Times, June 3, 1951, Sec. 7, p. 3.   Re-
printed in The Writer Observed.   New York:
World, 1956, pp. 199-201.

Canby, Vincent. "When Irish Eyes Are Smiling, It's
    Norman Mailer." New York Times, October 27,
    1968, Sec. 2, p. 15.

Carroll, Paul. "Playboy Interview: Norman Mailer."
    Playboy, January, 1968, pp. 69-72, 74, 76, 78,
    80, 82-84. Reprinted in Norman Mailer: The
    Man and His Work, ed. Robert F. Lucid. Bos-
    ton: Little, Brown, 1971, pp. 259-95. Excerpted
    in Existential Errands.

Christian, Frederick. "The Talent and the Torment."
    Cosmopolitan, August, 1963, pp. 63-67.

Cook, Bruce. "Angry Young Rebel with a Cause."
    Rogue, April, 1961, pp. 16-18, 76.

Dirnberger, Betsy. "The Norman Conquest." Other
    Voices (Elmira College), June, 1969, pp. 36-43.

Ellison, James Whitfield. "A Conversation with Norman
    Mailer [on Marilyn]. Book-of-the-Month Club
    News, August, 1973, pp. 4, 24.

Farbar, Buzz. "Mailer on Marriage and Women."
    Viva, October, 1973, pp. 74-76, 144, 146, 148,
    150, 152.

Gelmis, Joseph. The Film Director as Superstar.
    Garden City: Doubleday, 1970, pp. 43-63.

Grant, L. "Norman Mailer: Dialogue with the Non-
    mayor." Ramparts, December, 1969, pp. 44-46.

Griffiths, David. "TV Violence? It's a Sedative." TV
    Times, November, 1961, p. 18.

Kent, Letitia. "Rape of the Moon." Vogue, February 1,
    1971, pp. 134-35.

_____. "Films vs. Plays." Vogue, September 1,
    1972, pp. 200+.

Krassner, Paul. "An Impolite Interview." The
    Realist, December, 1962, pp. 1, 13-16, 18-23,
    10. Reprinted in abridged form in The Presi-
    dential Papers.

McCormack, Thomas, ed. Afterwords: Novelists on
    Their Novels. New York: Harper & Row, 1969.

Marcus, Steven. "The Art of Fiction XXII: Norman
    Mailer, An Interview." Paris Review, (Winter-
    Spring, 1964), pp. 28-58. Reprinted in Writers
    at Work: The Paris Review Interviews, Third
    Series, ed. George Plimpton. New York: Viking
    Press, 1968; and in Norman Mailer: A Collection
    of Critical Essays, ed. Leo Braudy. Englewood
    Cliffs, New Jersey: Prentice-Hall, 1972, pp. 21-
    41. Reprinted in a slightly different form in
    Cannibals and Christians.

Owitt, Trudy. New York, January 7, or February 5,
    1971.

[Smith, W. G.]. "Young American Rebel." Books and
    Bookmen, 7 (November, 1961), 28.

Stern, Richard. "Hip, Hell and the Navigator: An In-
    terview with Norman Mailer." Western Review,
    23 (Winter, 1959), 101-09. Reprinted in Adver-
    tisements for Myself.

Stone, I. F. "With Atheists Like Him Who Needs Be-
    lievers?" Christian Century (November 4, 1970),
    1313-17.

Stratton, Rick. Rolling Stone, Fall, 1974.

Stuart, Lyle. "An Intimate Interview with Norman
    Mailer." Exposé, December, 1955, pp. 1, 4.
    Reprinted as "Sixty-Nine Questions and Answers"
    in Advertisements for Myself.

Walker, Joe. "A Candid Talk with Norman Mailer."

Muhammad Speaks, June 20, 1969, pp. 11-12.

Wallace, Mike.   "Norman Mailer" in _Mike Wallace
    Asks_, ed. Charles Preston and Edward A.
    Hamilton.   New York: Simon & Schuster, 1958,
    pp. 26-27.

Weatherby, W. J.   "Talking of Violence."   _Twentieth
    Century_, 168 (Winter, 1964-65), 109-14.

Young, David.   "Norman Mailer on Science and Art."
    Antaeus (March, 1974), 335-45.

I. NONPRINT MEDIA

Fontaine, Dick, director. <u>Will the Real Norman Mailer Please Stand Up?</u> British Broadcasting Corp., 1968, [film].

Gelber, Jack. [Stage adaptation of] <u>Barbary Shore</u>, produced by Joseph Papp. New York: New York Shakespeare Festival Public Theatre (Anspacher), January 10-27, 1974 + 9 (preview) workshops. Reviewed in <u>New Yorker</u>, January 21, 1974, pp. 61-62.

Pease, Donald. [Lecture on <u>The Naked and the Dead.</u>] Deland, Florida: Everett/Edwards [30-40 minute tape cassette].

J. BIBLIOGRAPHIES

Adams, Laura. "Criticism of Norman Mailer: A Se-
    lected Checklist." Modern Fiction Studies, 17
    (Autumn, 1971), 455-63.

Braudy, Leo. "Selected Bibliography" in Norman
    Mailer: A Collection of Critical Essays. Engle-
    wood Cliffs, New Jersey: Prentice-Hall, 1972,
    pp. 180-85.

Curley, Dorothy Nyren, et al. , eds. A Library of
    Literary Criticism: Modern American Literature,
    Vol. II, 4th ed. New York: Frederick Ungar,
    1969, 270-78.

Downes, Robin Nelson. A Bibliography of Norman
    Mailer. Tallahassee: Florida State University,
    1957 [microcard only].

Gerstenberger, Donna and George Hendrick. The
    American Novel, 1789-1959: A Checklist of
    Twentieth Century Criticism. Denver: Alan
    Swallow, 1961, pp. 177-78.

Kaufmann, Donald L. "Selected Bibliography" in Nor-
    man Mailer: The Countdown. Carbondale:
    Southern Illinois University Press, 1969, pp. 177-
    84.

Leary, Lewis. Articles on American Literature, 1900-
    1950. Durham: Duke University Press, 1954,
    p. 199.

Lucid, Robert F. "A Checklist of Mailer's Published
     Work" in Norman Mailer: The Man and His
     Work. Boston: Little, Brown, 1971, pp. 299-
     310.

Malin, Irving, ed. Contemporary American Jewish
     Literature: Critical Essays. Bloomington:
     Indiana University Press, 1973, pp. 287-89.

Sadoya, Shigenobu. "A Bibliography of Norman Mailer
     [including Mailer in Japan, 1949-1972]." Studies
     of American Novels: Norman Mailer Number
     (Japan), 1 (May 25, 1973).

Shepard, Douglas. "Norman Mailer: A Preliminary
     Bibliography of Secondary Comment, 1948-1968."
     Bulletin of Bibliography, 29 (April, 1972), 37-45.

Sokoloff, B. A. A Bibliography of Norman Mailer.
     Folcroft, Pennsylvania: Folcroft Press, 1969.

ADDENDA

Adams, Laura. "Existential Aesthetics: An Interview with Norman Mailer." Forthcoming.

Brustein, Robert. "News Theater." New York Times Magazine, June 16, 1974, pp. 7, 36, 38-39, 44-45, 48. General.

Glicksberg, Charles I. "Norman Mailer: Salvation and the Apocalyptic Orgasm" in The Sexual Revolutions in Modern American Literature. The Hague: Nijhoff, 1971, pp. 171-81 et passim. General.

Graham, D. B. [Review of Bright Book of Life by Alfred Kazin.] Studies in the Novel, 5 (Fall, 1973), 404.

Hoerchner, Susan J. " 'I Have to Keep the Two Things Separate;' Polarity in Women in the Contemporary American Novel." Diss., Emory University, 1973 [The Deer Park and An American Dream].

Raleigh, J. H. "History and Its Burdens: The Example of Norman Mailer" in Uses of Literature, ed. Monroe Engel. Cambridge: Harvard University Press, 1973, pp. 163-86. General.

Solotaroff, Theodore. The Red Hot Vacuum and Other Pieces of Writing of the Sixties. New York: Atheneum, 1970, pp. 32-317 passim. General.

Zavarzadeh, Mas'ud. "The Poetics of Authenticity: The

Postwar American Nonfiction Novel." Diss. Indiana University, 1973 [The Armies of the Night and
others].

AUTHOR INDEX

Aaron, Jonathan 79
Adams, Laura vii-ix, xv,
  67, 68, 69, 73, 79, 83,
  84, 85-86, 87, 90, 93, 97,
  100, 101, 106, 109, 113,
  118, 120
Adams, Phoebe 44, 54, 63
Adelson, Alan M. 79
Aldridge, John W. 5, 46,
  51, 76, 79-80, 107, 108
Alexander, Sidney 37
Allen, Walter 80
Alpert, Hollis 37
Alter, Robert 80
Altherr, Thomas 109
Alvarez, A. 46, 51, 58, 80
Arlen, Michael J. 80
Arnavon, Cyrille 80
Auchincloss, Eve 113
Auchincloss, Louis 80
Avant, J. A. 69

Baker, Robert 54
Bakker, J. 80
Balakian, Nona 37
Baldwin, James 39, 107, 108
Bannon, B. A. 46
Barksdale, Richard K. 80
Barnes, Annette 66
Barrett, William 46
Baumbach, Jonathan 80-81,
  109
Beauman, Sally 74
Beaver, Harold 81
Beer, P. 66
Bell, Pearl K. 63, 81

Bellow, Saul 81
Berg, Louis 69
Bergonzi, B. 51
Berman, Ronald 81
Berry, John 66
Bersani, Leo 46, 81, 107,
  108
Berthoff, Warner 58
Bertrand, Suzanne 109
Bienen, L. B. 46
Bissett, Bill 46
Bittner, William 38
Blotner, Joseph 81
Bondy, François 81
Bone, Robert A. 39
Boroff, David 46
Boston, Richard 58
Bosworth, Patricia 81
Bourjaily, Vance 5
Bradner, Tim 81
Bragg, Melvin 113
Braudy, Leo 23, 39, 40,
  46, 48, 58, 59, 65, 67,
  79, 81-82, 83, 86, 100,
  102, 106-107, 115, 118
Bresler, Riva T. 38
Breslow, Paul 40
Brezianu, Andrei 82
Breit, Harvey 113
Bromwich, David 82
Bronson, Daniel Ross 109
Brookman, C. E. 82
Brooks, Charles W. 76
Brooks, John 38
Brooks, Peter 82
Brophy, Brigid 18, 66
Brower, Brock 82

INDEX OF MAILER'S WORKS

(Note: Only books, films and plays are indexed)

131